Sure Bet
Investing

IN SEARCH OF THE SURE THING

KENNETH R. TRESTER

Institute for Options Research, Inc.

Cover design by Sans Serif
Illustrations by Tim Sheppard, Olivia Trester, Robert Trester
Text design by Sans Serif

Trester, Kenneth R.
Sure Bet Investing /Kenneth R. Trester
p. cm.
Includes index.
ISBN 978-0-9604914-8-3

Published by:
Institute for Options Research, Inc.
1 (800) 407-2422
GoOptions.com

Contents

ILLUSION

The Not So Sure, Sure Bet Investing

The magical words for investors are "a sure bet". That is what many investors think when they buy a stock. This belief is either due to their own calculations or because a guru they follow says it is a sure bet. But real magic doesn't exist and neither does a sure bet. In fact, in most cases a "sure bet" is an oxymoron. If a sure bet were a sure thing, it wouldn't be a bet, for who would be on the other side of a bet they would be sure to lose. Yet like the medieval alchemist searching for the chemical combination that produces gold, the idea of a sure bet is irresistible, and what is irresistible makes the investor vulnerable. This vulnerability was made obvious in 2008.

2008 has taught us that few investments are predictable or safe. Six years of gains in the stock market disappeared. Many conservative bonds and preferred stocks dropped dramatically in value as the credit markets collapsed. Commodities that had been high flyers declined more than 50%. Real estate, once considered to be a sure bet, fell in price in 2006–2008.

In addition, we now have a vast number of mutual funds and hedge funds in the game, more than 10,000. These funds put much more pressure on the market and cause much more volatile moves. The VIX, a measure of volatility in the market, hit an all time high of almost 90% in 2008, when there were years when it was as low as 10%.

Even cash is risky. Cash, which is a safe haven during bad times, is not a good investment. On average the Fed increases the money supply 5% each year and that number is going up, so a dollar in 1990 is only worth less than 60 cents in 2010. Besides, any interest from the cash is taxed. You'll never keep ahead of inflation. In such a dangerous environment, it is difficult to find Sure Things.

Now investors, after losing wealth in 2008 investments which were once thought to be sure bets or at least safe havens, are rushing about looking for a place of greater safety. Are there places of greater safety? Are sure bets really an illusion? The answer to both questions is yes. Though a sure bet does not exist, one can still identify those investments or bets that come as close as possible to a sure thing; in other words, those FEW that APPROACH a sure bet. Medieval alchemists never chemically made gold, but they made other alloys that came close to the value of gold. Investors can increase the probability of approaching a sure thing, and that is the good news of this book. At the race track and in the market place, mindful of the dangers, we tried to find that one investment that day in and day out with our goal of a high probability play in a short period of time approached being sure to win.

However, before our search for these places of greater safety and profits, let's identify the obstacles. Identifying what the investors are up against is essential to avoiding the chimera of the sure thing.

REALITY

Know About the Smart Crowd

THE CROWD THAT CAN'T BE IGNORED

In most investment markets, the crowd is very smart, smarter than the most intelligent people in the crowd. It is the crowd that determines the stock price, and when stock prices drop dramatically for no reason, beware! Enron, World Com and Indy Mac all signaled that they were going belly up by their price action even though they denied having any critical problems. In fact, Indy Mac was not even on the FDIC's watch list of troubled banks. However, you knew the bank was in trouble when its stock price dropped below $2 a share. Hence, knowing the fundamentals was useless, but the technical action of the stock price told the whole story.

The stock price action will always tell you if a company is in trouble.

In horse racing, the crowd is so smart that it picks the winner of a race 33% of the time and has done so for over 100 years. In the game show "Who Wants to Be a Millionaire" when you asked the crowd a question, they were right over 90% of the time. Read the *Wisdom of Crowds* by James Surowiecki. It gives you more evidence that the wisdom of the crowd should not be ignored.

THE CROWD AND
THE DIFFICULT MARKET

Due to the fact that the crowd is so smart, it is difficult to win in the investment game. All stock prices are priced based on all the available information. The only time you get an opportunity for a bargain is when the market overshoots on the upside or downside. And determining when it will do that is difficult, particularly predicting the bottom of a market. For example, you are suppose to buy stock when there is blood in the street, but in 2008 there was blood in the street for a long time, and stock prices kept falling. Besides, it may take a long time for the bargains to pay off.

THE CROWD AND
THE EFFICIENT MARKET

A smart crowd means that the market is efficient, and it is hard to beat an efficient market. Because of the smart crowd, the greater majority of the time the stock market knows more than you do. Studies suggest that 80% of all market fund managers underperform the market averages. That proves that the market is efficient. If the professional on Wall Street can't beat the market, can you?

THE CONCLUSION

Because the very smart investment crowd has already discounted all present and likely future events into the stock price, trying to predict what a stock price or commodity price will do in the future is very difficult if not impossible. The future stock price is based on future events that no one knows at this time. Sure, you may call a stock move twice in a row or three, four or five times in a row, but that is not statistically significant and is caused more by luck than knowledge. In other words, you are competing with the crowd and only have feckless Lady Luck on your side.

Ignore the Smoke and Mirrors

As we try to make investment decisions, we are faced with a lot of smoke and mirrors. We have information overload, and the more information we get, the poorer our decision making. Most of this information is "noise" which contributes to incorrect analysis.

Journalists have a tendency to color news to substantiate their cause. In fact, sometimes the news is a big fat lie. The influence of the Global Warming Climate consortium and its cause is the worst example of this. Not only has that consortium and its cause had an unhealthy influence on journalists, it has had a significant influence on companies and countries throughout the world. When a scientist disagrees with the consortium's theory of global warming, it blackballs that scientist.

Its claim is that the people are causing global warming and that we will see dire consequences in the future. The only scientists brave enough to oppose the global warming theory are retired so that they can't lose their jobs. The Global Warming Climate consortium is so powerful that trillions of dollars are at stake. However, when you take a rational look at the issue, you discover that during the past ten years, the earth has been cooling rather than warming. The temperature of the water in the Arctic is the same today as it was in 1940. Yet there is so much false reiteration that few will oppose the global warming theory. The earth is 4.6 billion years old; our influence on the atmosphere is far smaller than most people think.

And now the EPA claims that carbon dioxide is a toxic substance and the government wants to tax anything that creates it. Well we all exhale carbon dioxide and plants need it to grow.

The Lunatics are now running the Asylum.

Finally, emails have been found that suggest that global warming scientists have been falsifying data to prove their case.

Here is another example where the experts are wrong and proves there are times when the market is very inefficient and the truth is hidden by smoke and mirrors.

In the late 1990's AOL was selling for a ridiculous price and I stated then in one of my lectures that AOL would need to get everyone in the world to subscribe to their service to warrant its stock price. Well, Time Warner paid that price—100 billion dollars for AOL. They spun off AOL in 2009 for only 2.5 billion dollars.

This is the kind of noise that makes it difficult to see and forecast the future. Most information that is dispersed is false and full of smoke and mirrors. As a result, it is best not to listen to financial analysts and journalists. The market acts randomly, and you would be far better off if you accepted this fact.

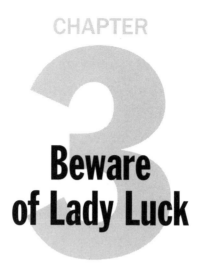

Beware of Lady Luck

Most people are mislead by Lady Luck.

THE SIGNIFICANCE OF "STATISTICALLY SIGNIFICANT"

We use the term *"statistically significant"*; this is a term used in the scientific community. For example, it tells us if a specific drug treatment has any meaningful effect on a patient. If the event is statistically significant, it will, in general, improve the health or reduce the symptoms of a medical condition. If not, it tells you that the treatment is probably based on random luck or has no significance. To be statistically significant, you need a large number of events.

However, in the investment world, we don't have a

large number of events to rely on. You pick five stocks in a row that go up in price; you think you are brilliant, but that is not a statistically significant result and could easily be caused by luck. Investors are sometimes hot and sometimes cold. Sure they will point to certain events to prove that their analysis was right, but probably it is all a matter of luck.

THE ELUSIVE WINNING SYSTEM

Finding a winning investment system is very difficult to do, for you will encounter long winning or losing streaks. This means the system you have discovered could be a losing system even though you have been winning or visa versa. That is why it is important to use science and mathematics as the basis of your methodology. (We'll deal with that later.)

THE WORTHLESS WINNING WORDS

When it comes to investing, testimonials and gurus are worthless. They might claim success but you can't know if what they are saying is based on luck or on the real thing. Unfortunately, the investment markets are a big gambling game, and the good results are usually based on luck. This tendency to give more credence to testimonials and winning gurus than is wise is especially true of the average investor.

THE RECKLESS LUCKY LOSERS

However, even the best investors in the world struggle. Hedge funds that are designed to provide the fund with protection against the volatility of the market suffered dramatically in 2008 with many going out of business. They surely were not sure bet investments. Many took highly leveraged risks and suffered accordingly. A hedge fund is designed to protect the investor from the risks of the market and charged high fees to manage these funds. But it turns out that they took more risks than regular mutual funds. Luck made them look attractive until recklessness did them in.

Long Term Capital, a large hedge fund failed in 1997 and almost took the whole economy down with it. And that hedge fund was run by top managers who had won a Nobel Prize.

THE CONCLUSION

Remember, as stated earlier, according to several studies almost 80% of mutual fund managers do not outperform the stock market. This indicates that much of the money manager's performance is based on Lady Luck. In *Fooled by Randomness* by Nassim Taleb and *(Mis) Behavior of Markets* by Benoit Mandelbrot and Richard Hudson, the investment markets are shown to move randomly and sometimes violently. The problem is, of course, that investors tie performance to skill when in many cases it is luck. A hot manager today is a cold manager tomorrow.

Understand Odds

Most investors don't realize how important luck is in determining their successes because many investors don't understand the laws of probability.

When you toss a coin, you have a 50% chance of getting a head or tail. If you flip a coin a thousand times you should get 500 heads and 500 tails. However on the journey to that point, the number of heads and tails will vary dramatically. In fact, the pattern looks like the price chart of a stock rather than a simple random process. In fact, Lady Luck has a big influence on what happens in the future.

In the casinos of Nevada there is an old chinese game called Keno. One of the bets is to select 15 numbers out of 20 numbers picked from 1 to 80. If you get the 15 numbers you win $100,000 for a $1 bet. What are your odds of hitting the 15 numbers? Your odds are 4.5 billion to 1. No has ever won this bet nor will they in the future.

When you buy options on stocks: What are your odds of winning? Most investors think they are much better than 50%. But their real odds are always under 50% and usually much lower than that. This tells you to know your odds before playing.

The same principle can be applied to the investment markets. A money manager can have a hot streak but in the long run is only right 50% of the time.

To determine the true odds of an event you need to run a computer simulation and that we will discuss in a future chapter.

CHAPTER

Roll Away
Crystal Balls

THE LAY OF THE LAND

Everyone tries to beat the market by trying to predict the future. The problem is that 90% of all investors are horrible failures at trying to predict short term moves in stocks, indexes and futures. As we have seen, even the professional shows a dismal record. Again remember that 80% of the stock mutual funds underperform the indexes and stock market averages year after year. This means that investing in an Index Fund where no management is involved is wiser than investing in a mutual fund of stocks, and there is no need to pay those management fees. This also tells you that future stock price actions are unpredictable. When the pros, who are paid hefty salaries, can't beat the averages, who can?

THOSE WHO USE CRYSTAL BALLS
EAT CHIPPED GLASS

THE EXPERTS

In fact, the brokerage firms spend millions and millions of dollars trying to find systems that will predict future stock and commodity prices, and their results have not been good. Even some of our top scientists have spent millions of dollars trying to develop a system for predicting stock prices and were unsuccessful. (However, they were able, after extensive research and testing, to develop a system to predict index prices. Check out the book, *The Predictors* by Thomas A Bass.)

THE TREND FOLLOWERS

As for trend followers, extrapolation can take you only so far because trends can be changed radically by chaos theory. Chaos theory states that small unrelated events can have a major impact on future events or trends. The unrelated small events are impossible to detect and their impact to foresee, much less plan for. Thus, trend followers will ultimately be disappointed.

THE DELUSIONAL ONES

Many investors I have encountered have a totally irrational view of their ability to predict the market. On numerous occasions, investors have asserted that they were 99% sure that the market would move up or down, and most of the time they have been wrong. In fact, some have become angry when I say that the markets approach randomness.

THE TECHNOLOGY

Over the next two decades as computers become more intelligent and even surpass human intelligence, most news events will be discounted in the markets long before they occur. Even now in the information age of the internet, this discounting occurs very rapidly. For example, the stock market moves six months before events occur, such as a recession bottom. Consequently, almost all future price moves are based on surprise news and events not available to the public. So don't think you can outwit the most advanced computers or the internet's collective wisdom. In other words, don't think you can predict the future. In fact, the more convinced you are that an event is likely to occur, the more likely that you will be wrong.

THE 60% RULE

When everyone believes in my prediction of the future, I know I'm in trouble. Based on this premise, I always apply my 60% rule to my predictions of what a stock or commodity or the market will do. That rule assumes I'll only be right 60% of the time, no matter how I feel about a position or projection. The rule forces me to design investment strategies that will pay off even if I am only right 60% of the time.

One of these strategies to invest in stocks is to buy a low-fee fund or an exchange-traded index such as the NASDAQ 100 (QQQQ) or the S&P 500 (SPY), and do this by dollar averaging; in other words, putting the same number of dollars in the market each month; do this in the third week of the month. Dollar averaging, a strategy that will come up again, enables you to participate in the long term growth of stocks without having to predict what will happen next week or next month, for once you try to time the markets, you are doomed. Remember, in the long run, you will probably only be right at the most 60% of the time, so adjust your strategies accordingly.

THE CONCLUSION

There are no crystal balls for predicting the markets. Academic studies strongly suggest that the markets move randomly. (Check out *A Random Walk Down Wall Street* by Button G. Milkier, now in its 8th edition.) And if the top brains and specialists, backed by millions of dollars, can't predict stock movements, you can't predict them. Therefore, again, the best way to approach the markets is to assume that they are random.

One situation I would look out for is when everybody loves a stock. If everyone loves a stock they own the stock and who will be left to buy it? Here it is wise to be a contrarian investor. Always do what everyone else is not doing.

"It is not for us to forecast the future but to shape it."
—Antoine de Saint-Exupery

Don't Hitch a Ride

Many investors are always in search of a free ride. They are looking for the guru that will lead them to the promised land or the system that is the Holy Grail. There is no system that will work all the time, and although there are analysts who are very good, they, too, will have their cold streaks.

One well-known advisor once predicted market moves eleven times in a row and then suddenly, and over a three year period, missed several major moves in the market. This is an example of why picking a truly good advisor can be quite difficult. Good performance is usually the result of Lady Luck, and if the markets are unpredictable, a guru in the long run will not provide much help.

Nor is there any surefire system. A system may work

for a while and then suddenly stop working. The trouble is that trading systems that are developed to generate profits are usually backtested, and backtested systems do not work. Here we are fooled again by Lady Luck. Backtested systems use inference or past stock action to develop the system. The problem is that the future may be far different than the past.

Being successful in the market depends on you! Too many investors seek out a guru who will make all their decisions; they will not take responsibility for their own actions. The only way to make it in the markets is to earn it. Use the wisdom of the experts, but make your own decisions and be willing to take the responsibility for those decisions.

One final comment regarding predictions. In 2010 after the 8.8 earthquake in Chile, the tsunami scientists gave a Tsunami Warning for Hawaii which means a tsunami would definitely hit Hawaii just like in 1960. Alarms went off every hour in Honolulu starting at 6 AM for the arrival at 11:30 AM. The beaches and highways were evacuated. Everyone was asked to stay at home. Well the tsunami never hit. This shows that even the best scientists have a lot trouble predicting things that MOVE!

Expect the Unexpected— Rogue Waves

In 2008 safe blue chip stocks turned out not to be safe, some dropping 90% in value. Real Estate was considered a sure bet but dropped dramatically in value. Such events seem to occur much more often than even the experts would expect. Events such as 9/11 or the election of a black US president were unthinkable just a few years before they occurred. These unexpected events make it very difficult to be a successful investor.

I call these events *rogue waves*. Rogue waves are ocean waves that are very high, about 100 feet high. Such waves, based on linear models, should only occur every 10,000 years. But based on recent history and observations, they occur much more often and even have hit some cruise ships. One ship disappears every week in the ocean. Once thought to be caused by human error or mechanical failure, many are now blamed on rogue waves. Rogue waves can appear anywhere in the ocean without warning.

In the investment market we see the same phenomenon. Rogue waves hit stocks all the time. They are news developments unexpected by anyone. Such events cause stocks to leap up or down in price.

Therefore, investing in the markets requires an investment that has a lot of upside gains, but minimal downside losses. Here options are the answer. And the options market is one of the places of greater safety that will be explored in the next and most important phase of this book: the search for the few investments that approach a sure thing.

REWARD

CHAPTER

The Search Begins

The search begins now for the least risky, most probable and profitable winner, and the quickest route and closest we can come to a sure thing.

Trying to find a sure thing in the midst of very efficient markets looks like an impossible task. However, in our search we found strategies where you can make bets that have a high probability of winning and that we could classify as close-to-sure bets.

As we started our search, we established that the bet must have three objectives:

1. A high probability of profit

2. A short timeframe—less than two months

3. A profit overall

To document these objectives, the probability of profit must have a long, long track record or be based on a mathematical formula. The testimonials of several people who say something works will have no relevance, for they are not statistically significant.

Beat the Horses!

At the Race Track

One place where we found a high probability of winning was in horse racing. Believe it or not, like the stock market, horse racing is an efficient market. In other words, the odds reflected on the tote board are a pretty accurate measure of the chances of a horse winning the race. This is based on a betting history going back over 100 years. As stated before, at all tracks for over 100 years the chances of the favorite winning the race was about 33%. Remember, the crowd is much more intelligent than you think.

But there is one tendency that distorts the odds a little. Horse players have a tendency to bet more on long shots than on low odd favorites, so betting on low odd favorites would be a better bet than long shots. Therefore, this market is not as efficient as you might think.

However, in the long run you would still lose, for there is a high percent taken out of the betting pool, usually around 18%. That is a lot to overcome.

THE WAY TO BEAT THE ODDS

One place where the odds are not listed is in the *place* and *show* pools. A place bet is a bet that a horse will run first or second. You win either way. A show bet is a bet that a horse will run first, second or third.

Just as in blackjack where if the count is good and there are a lot of high cards in the deck, you have the advantage; you can find an advantage in place and show betting. When a favorite low-odd horse has a smaller amount than is expected in the place or show pool, and If the amount bet in these pools is more than 20% less than the proper proportion for the favorite, you have an advantage. In addition, low-odd favorite horses have a high probability of placing or showing. For example, if the odds of a horse winning is 1–1, there is about a 71% chance of the horse placing and an 87% chance of the horse showing. Combine that with a place pool on a horse that has more than 20% less bet on him than the proportion of the win pool and you have a profitable bet.

These bets would meet all of the requirements of a Sure Bet formula: a profitable bet, a high probability of profit and instantaneous results; but try to get at least a 30% difference.

The problem you face is knowing when you have this 20% advantage. The only sure way to do this is to be the last person to make a bet, which, of course, is not possible at the track. Also, if you bet a large amount on a horse to place or show, you could destroy the advantage you had. Therefore, the best way to play this game is on the internet where you can bet at the last minute. You, also, need a fast way to determine if you have an advantage. We have developed a computer program that works on over 50% of the cell phones or on your computer. The program requires only 5 clicks to tell you if you have an advantage. Go to GoOptions.com.

ADDITIONAL HINTS

Try to only bet at the bigger tracks. Then you can bet more money, and it takes a lot more money to wipe out your advantage after you have made your bet.

Also, try to stay with favorites with odds at 1–1 or lower. One study suggests that place bets on horses with lower than 1–1 odds almost break even regardless of the place pool.

Play place or show on horses whose odds drop rapidly below 2 to 1 in the last 5 minutes before post time.

Why? this tells you this late money could be hot money that knows more about a horse than the public.

Also, the best tracks to play are the New York tracks such as Aqueduct or Belmont Park, for the breakage is lower. Your payoffs are better. Breakage is the extra amount that the track takes out of payoff prices. For example, if the payout price should be $2.96, the track will round down to $2.80 losing you 16 cents.

A SECRET RULE OF THUMB

Make sure to play horses to place where the amount bet on the horse in the place pool is less one third of the total place pool and the odds are less than 1–1.

Here you should be making a profitable bet. But your payoff each time will depend on the odds between the horse that runs first or second and your horse.

IN CONCLUSION

We have found our first Sure Bet System, a situation where there is not enough money bet on a low odd horse in the place or show pool compared to the win pool. Success with this system requires that you make bets at the last moment before the race starts or your advantage could disappear after you make the bet. So beware of the importance of time. Now by following this strategy, you may be able to beat the track!

In the Stock Market

REVIEW WHAT WE KNOW

As you know by now, the stock market, like horse racing, is usually an efficient market. Remember the intelligence of the crowd. Most stocks are fully discounted based on the information that is available. If a stock price moves, it moves because of new information or information unavailable to the public. That is why 80% of mutual fund managers are unable to beat the market, and why owning stocks can be dangerous.

Over a two month period in 2008 which we now refer to as the crash of 2008 most stocks lost 50% of their value.

During that period the stock market was more volatile than it has ever been. Many hedge funds that were designed to withstand such volatility went out of business or showed dismal performance.

One thing demonstrated is that there are no sure things in the stock market. How do you invest in a stock market with such risk?

Again we are faced with the question, if 80% of mutual fund managers can not beat the market, what can we do? And the answer is: play the market!

BUY THE INDEXES

In other words, bet on the whole market. Buy the *indexes* of the stock market. For example, you could buy the SPY (SPDR S&P 500 ETF Trust). This is an *Exchange Traded Fund* (ETF) that tracks the S&P 500 index and has a low management cost. Just as easily you can purchase other ETFs that cover the emerging markets. But you do not want to plow into these markets all at once. You must do dollar averaging.

DO THE DOLLAR AVERAGING THING

As mentioned above, every month put the same amount of dollars into the stock market by buying a low-fee index fund, as mentioned above, such as the SPY (S&P 500 index fund). Here you are diversified but still at the mercy of the whims of the market. However, by investing in bear markets when prices are low, something that most investors do not do, you have the advantage. Also, you won't be caught sitting on individual stocks that over many years have not shown gains, which was the case for a lot of people in 2008

MORE TO CONSIDER

One rule I would follow is to buy stocks two days before the end of each month, but avoid buying stocks in September. Why? Stocks tend to rise on the first four days and the last day of the month. But September is a bad month for the market. Most important, when looking for the closest you can get to a sure thing, you must always focus on protecting your capital.

And that brings us to the best vehicle with which to approach a sure thing: *options*. If you use our option system, there is a very big advantage to building your own stock and ETF portfolio rather than buying index funds.

11

On the Option Floor

THE ADVANTAGES

There are many advantages to options. One way to protect your capital but still be in the stock market is to buy options. In 2008 if an investor had invested in options with 10% of his capital, he may have lost up to 10% but still had 90% of his capital rather than losing 50% of his capital if he had merely invested the same money in stocks alone.

Another advantage to options is that you don't need a crystal ball. In fact, you don't have to be right about the market 50% of the time. Some option strategies win 90% of the time, regardless of what the market does. If you are an option buyer, one winner can pay for many losses. As a result, you can be wrong about the market most of the time and still be a winner. Also, options give you a lot of leverage; the 10% in options allows you to control up to 10 times the money invested in stocks, yet you are only risking 10% of your portfolio.

OKAY, WHAT ARE OPTIONS?

Options are like side bets on what a stock or index of stocks will do, but options only have a set time before they expire. In the appendix of this book, we have a Tutorial on options. Read it over and over again until you understand them, for options are one of our close-to-sure bet investments.

Options are considered dangerous investments by some, and they can be if you overdose or don't know what you are doing. But stocks can also be quite dangerous as many discovered in 2008. Also, much more can be lost on the stock market than in the options markets. When you follow our 10% rule, you limit your losses yet can participate in stock market gains.

BUYING OPTIONS

The key to selecting options in our 10% Game Plan is to buy long- term options that run as long as two and a half years. When you buy such options, you are in a sense renting the stock for two years. If the stock goes down, you lose the small amount that you paid for the options. Also, to have success using such options, you must pay a small price, set a profit goal and set a stop loss (a price where you exit the trade if the stock moves against you.)

For example, when General Electric is priced at 16, you could buy an option that has more than 2 years before it expires with a strike price of 17.5 for 2.6. In this case, you would risk $260 instead of $1600.

Our 10% formula can be very effective at preserving your capital and yet fully participating in the stock market. However, it is not a sure thing. Nevertheless, options can be used to go EVEN CLOSER to the sure thing. To do that, you need to learn about "option writing". That is what we will cover in the next chapter.

On the Option Floor— Writing Options— An Introduction

CLOSE TO THE SURE THING

The option game is the one place where you can win almost all of the time. Remember, an option is a side bet on what a stock, index, ETF or commodity price will do, but it is a bet that expires after a certain time. Buying options is easy to understand. It trades like a stock but is a depreciating asset, going down to zero by expiration if it is not across the stock's strike price.

For every buyer there is a *seller*, which we call a *writer*. The writer is like the casino. In a casino there are sports writers taking bets on sporting events and there are keno writers taking bets on keno. Now *you* can be a writer, taking bets on stock- *you can be an option writer.* In fact, most professional option traders I know are option writers rather than option buyers.

In order to write options, you need to get approval from your broker and have a certain amount in your account. Otherwise, option writing is just like buying options, except when you enter a position, you sell instead of buy to open. Then the price of the option goes into your account. Now you are obligated to pay up if the underlying stock goes "in-the-money"— across the strike price for a call option and below the strike price for a put option. For each point it goes " in-the-money", you lose $100 or one point.

It is as simple as this: take $10 out of your pocket and give it to your wife or husband. Here you are the option buyer and your partner is the option writer. That $10 is now in the partner's hands.

With option writing you can create strategies that win 90% of the time. However, can option writing create long term profits? The answer is yes! That is where probabilities and theoretical values come into play. The value of options can be measured mathematically. An option can be overvalued or undervalued. This tells you the option markets are not efficient all the time and gives the option writer opportunities.

Altogether, for a Sure Bet Play, you need a high probability of profit, you must only play overvalued options, and you need to write shorter-term options. Determining the probability of profit can be measured scientifically with a computer simulation program, and measuring the fair value of an option can be done using a pricing model such as the Black and Scholes Model, which won a Nobel Prize. So, from a theoretical standpoint, our goals can be met, and they are:

1. High probability

2. Profitable results

3. Short time frame.

THE JARGON, THE PROBLEM, THE ADVANTAGE

Call options are entitled "calls" because they give the buyer the right to call the stock from you. If you write put options, you are giving the buyer the right to "put" or sell the stock to you. When you write (sell) options without owning the stock, you are a "naked writer". If you write calls on 100 shares of a stock that you own, you are a "covered writer".

The problem you face with naked option writing is that you have high or unlimited risk. As the option writer, you are paying off if the option pays off for the buyer. With puts, if you do not mind owning 100 shares of the stock at the strike price, this is okay.

You win with "out-of-the-money" options (options where the strike price is above the stock price for calls and below the stock price for puts) if the underlying stock price stays where it is, moves up or down slowly or moves in your direction. You lose only if the underlying stock or ETF makes a big move against you.

Furthermore, the writer has one big advantage. You can close the position at any time by buying back the option. In a sense, the casino can close the doors at any time.

Reminder: Read the Tutorial!

On the Option Floor— Writing Options Conservatively

COVERED CALL WRITING

There are many ways to play this game, and they vary according to their risk. The most conservative are "covered call" writing and "naked put" writing. These could be Win-Win Option writing strategies, which means that they are strategies that win regardless of what happens. Let's start with "covered call" writing.

Covered call writing, as explained before, is where you write a call option but also own the stock or ETF. Covered call writing is a way to generate more income for your portfolio, but it has its drawbacks. For one, by owning the stock, you limit your upside potential, yet you still have extensive downside risk. The bear market of 2000–2002 and 2008–2009 demonstrated that risk. Therefore, you should use covered writing carefully.

I use it as a way to take profits on a stock portfolio. For example, if you owned Lockheed Martin (LMT) at 52 and wanted to take profits if it hit 60, you could write a 60 call on LMT. If LMT surpassed 60 before expiration and is assigned (exercised), you lose the stock, but that was your intention in the first place, so you win. On the other hand, if the stock does not hit your target, you at least collect the premium from writing the call. So, in either case you have made a winning move. By the way, if you change your mind when LMT hits 60 and want to keep the stock, just buy back the call and close your obligation.

NAKED PUT WRITING

Naked put writing can also be a win-win proposition. It is a way you can buy the underlying stock, ETF or futures. By writing far out-of-the-money puts, you can attempt to buy the underlying stock at much lower prices.

One of my friends who made millions of dollars in the stock market loves to write far out-of-the-money naked puts, but only on stocks that he would love to own at much lower prices. To get enough premium from this activity, he will in many cases write longer term options, again trying to get stocks at 30% to 60% below the present price. He views this activity as a win-win situation, for if the stock falls below the strike price of the put he has written and he is assigned the stock, he is delighted. That is just what he wanted. On the other hand, if the option expires worthless, he gets a consolation prize, the premium from writing the put. In both cases he wins.

Here is another example. If you want to buy 100 shares of GE at 12.5 when it is 16, you could write (sell) the Jan 12.5 put for 1. If GE is at or below 12.5 at expiration, you will get the stock at 11.5 (12.5 − 1 = 11.5). If the stock is above 12.5, you still win, for you received $100 when you wrote the option.

Major corporations do naked put writing with the same purpose in mind. They use naked put writing as part of *share-buy-back* programs in an attempt to buy their shares at lower prices and at the same time to collect put premiums as they wait to get these prices.

Naked put writing is an excellent way to build a portfolio of stocks and ETFs. And when you select plays that win 85% to 90% of the time, you will earn a lot of income waiting to buy the stock at lower prices.

Try to find stocks that show good value and good growth potential over the next few years. Then find out-of-the money puts to sell (write) on those stocks. Here you are trying to buy stocks when they are ON SALE at lower prices and you get paid waiting to get those stocks.

On the Option Floor— The Risks and the Rewards of Playing It Naked

You have received your first application of option writing with the conservative, defensive strategies of covered option writing and naked put writing. Now let's pull out some of the stops and play a far more exciting game. Let's Play It Naked.

Up to this point, we have been discussing the position of the covered option writer who covers his option writing risk by owning the underlying common stock. He gains only part of the benefit of option writing by playing it safe and maintaining a conservative defense; he can not reap all the various profits available to the option writer.

In contrast, "playing it naked" is a method that

reaps all of the benefits and potential profit of the sport of option writing. The naked option writer writes options without the common stock or ETF covering his position. Although there are some substantial risks in this game, which we will explain later, let us first look at some of the important benefits to be gained.

ADVANTAGES OF
NAKED OPTION WRITING

1. *The Potential Rewards Are Outstanding*

   To the professional option player, naked option writing is the Cadillac division of the options market. The profit potentials here are greater than in any other segment of the options market. The skilled and disciplined naked option writer can generate from a 50% to a 100% return annually on his investment and normally can do this consistently over a long period of time. The naked writer can become a "man for all seasons", confronting numerous opportunities in bull, bear, and nomad market conditions.

2. *The Odds of Winning Are in the Writer's Favor*

   You will discover, if you decide to participate in this Grand Prix of the options market, that when you run a naked option writing portfolio, a high percentage of your positions will be winners. If you pick the right options, 80% of your positions are likely to come out profitable and only 20% will be losers. In other words, the odds are stacked in your favor. Naked option writing is probably the only game in town where the investor truly has an advantage over the rest of the market.

Consider this analogy. The casino operator who offers roulette, craps, and blackjack to patrons who visit his casino is similar to the option writer. The casino operator backs the bets of the gaming customers. He pays off when the customers are big winners and takes in profits when they are losers. The casino operator has a slight advantage in each game.

In roulette, for instance, he has approximately a 5% advantage over the gaming customer. The option writer is in a similar position, but his advantage is better than 5%.

The academic studies and research that have been done so far have indicated that the option writer (seller) actually has a 10% to 20% advantage over the option buyer (if he writes overvalued options). The option writer like the casino owner, provides the option buyer with a market in which to speculate, in which to gamble. For this service, the option writer receives better odds.

The major advantage that gives him this percentage edge is TIME. The option buyer bets that the stock will go up significantly when he buys a call. But the option writer wins under all other stock price conditions. The call option writer is a winner even if the stock moves up too slowly because as time passes, the premium that the option writer receives from the option buyer for backing his bet depreciates, moving into the pocket of the option writer.

The option writer has two important factors in his favor:

1. He does not require that the underlying stock price move to make a profit.

2. He is continually making a profit as the option shrinks in value with passing time.

The option writer who writes strictly naked options with no hedges, no stock and no long options to cover his naked positions is attempting to maximize these two advantages.

For example, an option buyer purchases a Pfizer Jan 40 call at 3, with three months to run. The stock price is at 37. There is actually no real value in that option at the time the option buyer purchases the option. The only value the option holds is time value. The $300 option price goes to the option writer. In order for that option to take on any real value at all, the stock price must move above 40. For the option buyer to break even at the end of that three-month period, the stock price must be at 43. If the Pfizer stock price is below 40 at the end of the three-month period, the option will expire worthless. The writer will have made $300 less commissions, and the buyer will have lost $300.

Therefore, the profit parameters for the option writer would read—by the end of January. If the stock price is below 43, he wins. Conversely, if the stock price is above 43, the option buyer wins. However, the option writer starts with the advantage because when the option was purchased, the stock was 6 points below the break-even point for the buyer. Actually, the option writer starts with a profit; he has $300 and 6 points to work with before the time period begins.

3. *Success Does Not Depend on Predicting Stock Price Behavior*

The option writer, unlike the option buyer, is not required to predict the exact extent of a stock price move. Because the option writer begins the game with the odds stacked in his favor, he can afford a wide margin of error in measuring and predicting what a stock price will do in the future.

In fact, there are many theorists who believe that it is impossible to predict the price action of a stock in the future. They consider the stock market a random walk down Wall Street. As you operate your naked option writing portfolio, although you should not ignore the trend of the market or a stock, you can partially adopt a random walk theory. Even if you write an option and the stock moves in the wrong direction, if the move is slow enough or short enough, you can still come out ahead.

Remember that in our scenario regarding the price action of a specific stock, a stock can move up significantly, can move up a little, can stay where it is, can move down a little or can move down a lot. Thus when you are writing calls, the only time that you will lose is if the stock moves up significantly during the period that you back that contract. If you are writing puts, the only time that you lose is if the stock moves down significantly.

4. *The Theoretical and Academic Arguments Supporting Naked Option Writing Are Excellent*

Before the existence of the options exchanges, naked option writing was practiced by a select few in the old over-the-counter (OTC) market and was a far more dangerous game than writing listed options today. The OTC option writer faced numerous obstacles that made it unfeasible for most investors to enter that game. Yet, even with these dangerous pitfalls, studies of the old OTC market show encouraging results that support the more advantageous position of the option writer today.

The opinions of the experts indicate that almost 65% of all options in the OTC market were never exercised (expired without value). In the old OTC market when an option was written or sold, the stock price was right at strike price. This is not true today. Now you can write options where the stock price is a great distance from the strike price. We refer to these as "out-of-the-money" options. In the old OTC market, normally the only type of option that was written was an "at-the-money" option, an option in which the strike price and stock price were identical.

Even in the OTC options market and even when options were at-the-money, the writer had a slight advantage because only 35% of all options were exercised. These performance claims are backed by a considerable body of research. In the book, *Strategies and Rational Decisions in the Securities Options Market*, the authors, Burton G. Malkiel and Richard E Quandt, reported that their research conducted from 1960–1964 proved that writing OTC options on a random basis, without any judgments or safe-guards, was indeed a profitable game in all cases.

In contrast those who bought during that period, regardless of what strategy was used, always ended up with a negative result. Therefore, they discovered that the writing of naked call options was one of the optimum strategies available in the options market, generating over a 10% annual return. With such encouraging results on a random basis, imagine what the returns would be if a little skill, a little knowledge and the proper timing were added to this investment model

Another study that indicated the feasibility of option writing came from the book, *Beat the Market* by Sheen Kassouf and Ed Thorp. The results of their strategy was based on the shorting of warrants on the Stock Exchange, which is almost the same as writing call options on the Options Exchange. Through the use of track records and some sound theoretical and academic studies, Kassouf and Thorp proved that the short selling of warrants can provide a high and consistent profit when the investor also uses a hedging strategy. Though they did not discuss writing warrants without any type of hedge, the maximum flow of profit came from *that* technique.

Finally, documentation verifies that in the first

year and a half of operation of the CBOE, (Chicago Board Option Exchange) only 10% of all options in the new option markets had any real value when their lives expired.

DISADVANTAGES OF NAKED OPTION WRITING

When we look at the disadvantages of naked option writing, one stands out clearly above all others: RISK. There is unlimited risk when writing naked call options, and extensive risk when writing naked puts, the risk that the underlying stock price will move through and far above or below the option strike price. This highly publicized risk scares many investors away from the naked option writing game, and many who have played in this unusual game have been wiped out by the volatility and action of naked options. Regulatory agencies, brokers and many option players cringe when you talk about naked options; there is more fear floating around about naked options than about any other investment vehicle available today. But, although a definite risk does exist in the naked option writing market, this risk is usually exaggerated.

To show why this is true, let us examine these possible risks of naked option writing in detail and decide which actions to take to guard against them.

1. *The Risk of Not Being Covered by Common Stock*

We have already mentioned the unlimited risk that the option writer has when he is not covered by the common stock. Here is an example. If you were to write five call options on Pfizer with a strike price of 40, and Pfizer were to move through the 40 strike price in an upward direction, you would be responsible for delivering 500 shares of Pfizer to the buyer if at any time he chose to exercise his options. Your risk for each point that Pfizer moves above 40 will be $100 per option position that you hold. In the case of the five Pfizer calls, you would have $500 of risk for each point that Pfizer moved above the strike price of 40. If Pfizer were to move from a price of 40 to 45, your actual loss would be $500 per option for the 5 points that the stock moved, which comes out to $2,500.

2. *Negative Risk-Reward Ratio*

A second related risk that scares many a player away is the possibility of a negative risk-reward ratio. In our first example of Pfizer, we mentioned that the maximum amount that the option writer could gain by writing a Pfizer Jan 40 at 3 was $300 profit. On the other hand, his counterpart, the option buyer, has unlimited profit potential from the option position. If the Pfizer price were to move

37 to 60 within a short period of time, the option buyer would generate a profit of $1,700, less commissions, on his $300 investment. The option writer, who only had $300 to gain, would lose $1,700 on the naked option writing position. Consequently, the risk-reward ratio in this example does not look very attractive to the naked option writer.

However, there are two counter-arguments in favor of the naked option writer regarding this risk:

1. The probability that Pfizer or any stock would make such a large move within a short period of time is small. The likelihood that the buyer will be a winner in his option positions is normally minimal. It is important for you to consider the probabilities with any stock in order to reduce the negative risk-reward scenario that can occur to the naked option writer.

2. The shrewd naked option writer rarely owns an option that has become so fat as to provide a big reward for the option buyer. He will usually never allow such a negative risk-reward scenario to develop. The professional naked option writer will have left that option position long before this occurs. One of the beauties of the options markets is the ability to close out a transaction at any time.

Here the all-important quality of DISCIPLINE comes into play. When the stock moves in the wrong direction, moves through your parameters, which you must always set before entering a position, you as a naked option writer must immediately extricate yourself from that position by buying back the option.

The tools to avoid the risks will be discussed further in a future chapter.

WAR STORIES

Before you become too enthusiastic about naked option writing, be warned that this game is for high risk players ONLY. Sometimes those theoretical unlimited risks do become a reality. In the 1980's, leveraged buy-outs of one company by another were the rage. Such events caused dramatic overnight changes in a stock price. Kennecott Copper common stock price rose almost 30 points overnight when Standard of Ohio bought them out. If you were a Kennecott naked call writer, there was no way to exit your position before the damage was done. You would have taken a 30 points ($3000) loss on each call that you had written. The takeover rage has died down, for junk bond financing has gone out of favor, but takeovers will occur in the future, and they are the naked stock option call writer's greatest danger.

On the other side of the coin, naked put writing has dangers of its own. Stocks may drop sharply when a news event or negative earnings report is published and institutions rush out of the stock. If the stock gaps down in price, the naked put writer can not limit his losses and will take a bad hit. Here is a case where you can not close the casino door to minimize your losses.

How can you protect yourself from such losses? DIVERSIFY! Maintain extremely small positions in each stock. Then if you do take a big hit, you will limit your loss to just a few options. In addition, avoid stocks that are takeover targets or those vulnerable to a surprise move, such as some over-the-counter stocks. Also, keeping diversification in mind, write naked put options on *low-priced* stocks that you would like to own because your maximum risk is then small.

One war story that demonstrates the risk of naked writing involves index options. Index options seem an ideal candidate for option writing. Index options tend to be overpriced; they move slowly and are not vulnerable to takeovers or surprise earnings reports. Before the crash of 1987, naked index option writing was a lucrative game. Rumor has it that one investor started with $15,000 two years before the crash and made it grow (writing naked index options) to $750,000 before the crash occurred. But on the day of the crash, he lost the $750,000 and two million more that he did not have.

Before the crash, the Major Market Index (XMI) was priced at $520 (520 × 100 = $52,000), and one XMI 480 put was priced at 1 ($100). If you would have sold the 480 put, you would have received $100, and the XMI would have to drop 40 points, or 200 points on the Dow, to get into trouble. On the day of the crash, the XMI dropped to 380. How much have you lost? First, the XMI was 100 points in-the-money (480–380 = 100), so the intrinsic value of the put was 100 ($10,000). But due to fear (during the crash) to buy back that put on the exchange, you would have had to pay $200 ($20,000). If you had sold five options, your losses would have been close to $100,000.

Many small investors who were writing naked index options were caught in this disaster and saw the value of their accounts disappear. In addition, many investors owed their brokerage firms huge amounts of money from their writing losses. The brokerage firms ate most of these losses and hence lost millions. Such events turned the brokerage firms dead against naked writers. So now many firms will not allow naked writing, even if it is conservative put writing, to buy the underlying stock.

In addition, now the exchanges can stop the trading

of index options when the market drops or rises extensively during the same day. Such action makes it quite dangerous to write naked index options, for you may be prevented from closing your position if the market moves against you.

Stock options don't have this problem. With stock options the exchanges won't prematurely close when the market drops or rises extensively; of course, you can always buy or sell the underlying stock to cover your position if you are unable to deal in the option.

However, remember, as previous examples show, stocks, even blue chip stocks, can be hit by rogue waves and sweep your profits and more away before you can respond and protect yourself. In 2007 Wellcare Health Plans dropped from 120 to 30 overnight. In 2008, Bear Stearns dropped from 30 to 2 overnight. Naked put writers suffered dramatic losses with these moves, for they could not get out of their positions.

MARGIN REQUIREMENTS FOR NAKED OPTION WRITING

The naked option writer, unlike the covered option writer, must put up a certain amount of cash or other form of collateral for each option position that he establishes. This cash or collateral (referred to as a margin requirement) guarantees to the Exchange and the brokerage house that the writer will make good on his contract if the underlying stock suddenly moves in the wrong direction.

There are many firms who continue to live in ignorance and thus set up ridiculous requirements for naked option writers, requiring an initial deposit running from $25,000 to $100,000. There are, however, brokerage houses that are far more reasonable and provide minimal margin requirements and initial deposits to enter this exciting game. These are the types of firms you should seek out if you wish to take on the supreme challenge of the options market.

During the first two years of existence of the Options Exchange, the margin requirements were minimal in many CBOE member firms, giving the naked option writer significant leverage and, therefore, significant return on investment during that bear market period. Portfolios multiplied within weeks; gains of 1,000% to 2,000% were not unusual. Pressure from the SEC, the New York Stock Exchange, and its member firms has forced margin rules upward to a point where now, in order to write a naked option, you must put up, in the form of cash or collateral, 20% of the value of the underlying common stock.

For example, if you were to write an option on Xerox when Xerox was selling for $60 a share, you would have to put up a deposit of 20% of the value of the 100 shares of Xerox stock, which comes out to $1,200. This $1,200 margin requirement would be increased or decreased, depending on how far the stock price was from the strike price of the option you have written.

A major obstacle that the professional option writer faces is his ability to get a high enough return on investment for each position he enters. The margin requirements will be the greatest hurdle that he encounters in meeting this challenge, so he must continually attempt to identify naked options that require a minimum amount of margin.

NAKED OPTIONS AS A DEFENSE

Naked options, combined with common stock, fixed securities, convertible bonds or long option purchases provide protection and consistent returns. Some money managers are beginning to discover this fact and use naked option writing to cushion their portfolios from the uncertainty of the stock market.

For example, a money manager with a portfolio consisting of common stock or fixed securities might consider taking 10% of his portfolio and just write naked options with that portion. Writing naked puts and calls will provide a cushion against risk in both bull and bear markets and provide excellent results in nomad markets. Overall, this approach to the market is defensive, providing some protection to such a portfolio.

CONCLUSION

You now know the advantages and disadvantages of naked option writing. You know the hurdles you have to get over and the protection naked options writing affords a portfolio. Most of all, you know some of the horror stories of naked option writing and how devastating the losses can be when writing naked puts and calls on stocks or indexes. At the same time, you have been given some strategies that can protect you or limit your risk. However, when you are writing naked options, more guidance is needed and that is what the next chapter gives you.

CHAPTER

On the Option Floor— The Secrets of Playing It Naked

A WARNING!

Naked call writing is not recommended, for most investors—there is too much risk.

Naked put writing is only recommended if you plan to buy the stock, or don't mind buying the stock or ETF, or if you are writing puts on low priced stocks. However, if you plan to buy stock, always write puts

THE TEN SECRETS OF NAKED OPTIONS

As we disclose more of the secrets of the mysterious art of naked option writing, you will learn that they are based on simple and concrete principles.

As a naked option writer, you must develop and adhere to a solid strategy that has several lines of defense built in to protect and control the numerous risks that will surround you. You must have the discipline to follow the controls that you set up; you must follow your strategy; you must follow your defensive measures. Most important of all, you must be able to "pull the trigger" and take a loss gracefully. Only by using the following guidelines will you protect yourself from the numerous risks that scare many brokers, brokerage houses and option players from this game. However, if you follow these guidelines, you will reap the rewards that this game offers.

Let's begin by looking closely at the TEN SECRETS OF NAKED OPTION WRITING!

1. *Set a Bailout Point and Use It*

A bailout point is the price or the point in your strategy at which you want to buy back your naked positions in order to limit your losses. This stock price or option price at which you want to bail out of your position is the most important segment of your naked option writing strategy. With naked options you must have a set of safeguards as a defense to limit your losses and control the tremendous risks. You must have a point at which you will bite the bullet if your naked options go astray.

Remember, the outstanding feature of the options markets is the right that you have as a

option writer to go into the market at any time and buy back your naked options, thereby limiting all possible future losses. Setting a bailout point is a way of insuring that you use this right when the price hits the parameters that you have set up.

How do you bail out of a position? There are actually two approaches that you can take to limit your losses in a naked option position.

The first requires an option player of strong mind and body, an option player with outstanding discipline and nerves of steel. When the underlying stock price touches his bailout parameter, this type of an option player can afford to have the prerogative of voluntarily moving into the market and buying back his options at his own discretion. Upper most in the option player's mind when he carries out this process, should be that if he does not bail out at this point, there is a chance that he will lose everything. When you are running a naked option writing portfolio, your overall goal should be to stay in the game, and the only way you will ever stay in the game to participate in the eventual profits is by bailing out whenever your loss parameters are touched.

The second approach requires a Stop-Loss Order. This approach to bailing out of an option position has been designed for the option player who is not as experienced or feels that he doesn't want to rely totally on his own discipline. Just think of jumping out of an airplane as analogous to taking a loss in a naked option position. If you feel that you can easily parachute out of that airplane every time without a push, then you may have the discipline necessary to voluntarily move out of your option positions. On the other hand, if it might be easier for you to receive a little push when you jump out of that plane, then the use of a "stop-loss order" to bail you out of your option positions would probably be the wiser alternative.

Remember, it might be easy now to say, "Yes, I'll voluntarily cover my naked shorts and buy my options back when the underlying stock hits my loss parameters." But when investors actually get into the midst of the battle, they have a hard time making decisions that involve taking losses. They will not bite the bullet; they would rather wait and hope that the stock will change direction. Their emotions take over, and they have illusions that are totally unrealistic; they start to build stories around why their stock will not move any further. All these factors can come into play, and the investor must win over these emotions, or else in most cases he will lose. Therefore, the stop-loss order might be a much wiser alternative than attempting to jump out of that plane voluntarily.

What is a "stop-loss order" A stop-loss order is a special order placed on the Options Exchange whereby your naked option position will be covered (bought back) under one of two conditions:

1. If the underlying stock price reaches a certain price, which you have set as your bailout price

2. If the option price reaches a predetermined price

I strongly suggest that you use the first of these.

Attempt to set the point at which you have decided to limit your loss by using the stock price's action rather than by using the option price. Option prices move in erratic patterns, and in many cases they may become extremely inflated, even though the stock price has not moved accordingly. Your major concern as a naked option writer is where the stock price is going to end up. Consequently, you should select a stop-loss that is contingent upon the stock price if possible.

For example, let's say that you wrote a Xerox Jan 60 call option when the stock was at 50, and you set a bailout point at 58. This order would indicate that if the Xerox price reached 58, your option would immediately be bought back and your position would be closed out. The order to buy back your option would be a market order.

The market order feature of a stop-loss order is the only real disadvantage to using stop-loss orders in a options market. Market orders in the stock market usually work out well, but on the Options Exchange, a market order can be dangerous. Some options trade in thin markets. In other words, they have low liquidity, and market orders in thin markets can be costly experiences. On the floor of the exchange, market makers love to take advantage of market orders when there are few buyers and sellers around. But now there are limits on the spread between the bid and asked price, so market orders work out better.

Note: Several options exchanges and brokerage houses do not accept option stop-loss orders.

2. *Write Naked Call Options in Bear Markets; Write Naked Put Options in Bull Markets.*

This secret of naked option writing is self-explanatory. To improve your probability of winning this game, it is far wiser to write calls when the stock prices in general are moving down and to write puts when stock prices are moving up. This strategy puts the odds in your favor. However, because of the inherent advantage the naked option writer holds, naked call options during bull markets can be profitable as can naked put writing during bear markets.

3. *Write Naked Calls on Underlying Stocks That Are in a Major Down Trend; Write Naked Puts on Underlying Stocks That Are in a Major Up Trend*

Your profits will be much greater in the naked option writing game if you write calls when the underlying stock is moving downward and, if you write puts, when the underlying stock is moving upward. The best way to project this type of price behavior is to look at the underlying trend of each of the "optionable" stocks. Never buck a strong up trending stock, or in Wall Street parlance, "Don't fight the tape."

4. *Select Stock Candidates with a Low Price Volatility.*

While the option buyer always hunts and pecks for options on stocks that are extremely volatile, the option writer loves stocks that don't move in a narrow range because the option writer always has time working in his favor. The slower a stock price moves, the more money he makes. Options with slow moving underlying stocks will depreciate to zero before the stock ever reaches a bailout point. Unfortunately, the stocks with the highest volatility maintain the highest and fattest premiums for option writing, so the option writer must attempt to find options with low volatility and correspondingly high premiums (time value) when possible.

5. *Diversify; Maintain at Least Four Different Option Positions with Different Underlying Stock*

You've heard this before; naked option writing with its extreme risks requires diversity. Remember, one of your overall goals is to stay in the game, and the best way to do that is to avoid betting all your money on one horse. Although the odds are heavily in your favor, losers can put you out of the game if everything you have is bet on one position. Finally, maintain very small positions in each stock so that a takeover does not nail you with devastating loss.

6. *Write Puts and Calls That Are At Least 15% Out-of-the-Money.*

    I believe that when you are carrying out a naked option writing program, the only options you should ever consider as writing candidates are those that have no real (intrinsic) value, that are not in-the-money. Use only those options that are out-of-the-money, that have only time value. In fact, select options that are *significantly* out-of-the-money, so that it will take a strong move in the stock (a move that normally would not occur in a two or three month time period) to hit your parameters. These out-of-the-money options, which require a major move in the stock to take on a any value at all, have a low probability of ever being exercised or of ever having any real value, and this low probability is a strong advantage to the naked writer.

7. *Write Naked Options with No More Than Three Months Left in Their Life*

    Remember that as an option approaches expiration, its rate of depreciation normally increases, especially in the last month. Consequently, these are the times to write naked options. You will receive a higher rate of premium in the last three months of the option than at any other time in its life. The shorter the time before expiration the better.

8. *Write Options That Are At Least 25% Overpriced According to Their Fair Value.*

One of the most important secrets to successful naked option writing is to write only options that have been overpriced by the market, options for which the buyer is paying too much. This will add insurance to your profit potential and is an important key to successful option writing. Make sure that the options you plan to write are at least 25% over the fair value.

9. *Write Options Against Treasury Bills.*

I've mentioned before that when writing options, you must put up a margin requirement. That margin requirement can be in the form of cash or securities. It can also be in the form of Treasury Bills. If it is in the form of securities, you can only use the loan value of the securities. However, Treasury Bills are treated just like cash, and this is a one major advantage of using them. Treasury Bills will generate from 2% to 10% annually, depending on the money market, and this will be an added dividend to your option writing portfolio. Not only will you generate the profit from option writing, but also you will generate the return each year from your Treasury Bills.

Most brokerage houses place your credit balance in the money market so you will still earn interest if you don't have Treasury Bills.

10. *Maintain a Strict Stock/Option Surveillance Program.*

Watch your stock and option prices like a hawk. Monitor every move that the stock and option prices make during the periods of time that you are holding these naked option positions.

The professional naked option writer will keep a close eye on the price action of the underlying stock and will cover a position, bail out of a position or buy back a position if there is a change in the trend of the underlying stock. He will also take profits early when the option shrinks in value quickly because of an advantageous stock price move, or he may take action when the options become extremely undervalued, according to the value of the stock price.

The closer you carry out a surveillance program, the better your profits will be and the smaller your losses will be.

This surveillance program should also contain a continuous writing feature that is best described as a method of reinvesting funds into new naked option writing positions as profits are taken. This process is similar to compounding interest in your bank account, although in a naked option writing account, the profits that are being compounded are much greater. By continually reinvesting in new positions and by actively taking profits when they develop, your portfolio will grow at a far faster rate than is possible if you maintain a static program of waiting until options expire. There is a tremendous difference between an active naked option writing program and a static one where no action occurs until the expiration date arrives, The compounding of profits in a naked option writing portfolio can be a significant factor in providing outstanding returns.

A WARNING is appropriate here; make sure that you always have your naked option positions mapped before you enter them. Attempting to design and implement strategies that are not displayed on paper in black and white is a dangerous game especially with naked options.

Now you have the secrets of naked option writing. Take them seriously and use them wisely. Pay particular attention to setting a bailout point and diversifying. The bailout point is your parachute, and diversification, your net.

On the Option Floor— Writing it Defensively

THE NAME OF THE GAME

As you know by now, when it comes to option writing, not just naked option writing, defense is the name of the game. It has been emphasized that unless you want to buy a stock for put writers and/or sell a stock you own for call writers, you MUST set a stop-loss price where you will buy back the option. But even THAT may not give you enough protection, for the stock price could gap up or down, giving you a much greater loss.

CHEAP, FURTHER OUT-OF-THE-MONEY OPTIONS

Further defense is necessary because you must protect yourself from such events. One way to do that is to *buy* a much cheaper option that is further out-of-the-money than the one you're going to *write*, usually 2-1/2 to 5 points further out. If you still have a good credit, you have a good play. This is called a credit spread

INDEX FUNDS AND ETFs

Another protection is to write options on index funds or ETFs. Though there are hazards for naked writers as discussed earlier, these funds are much less likely to gap up or down in price.

CREDIT SPREADS

The best way to build protection into your position is with credit spreads. When you write naked calls or naked puts and do not own the underlying stock or ETF, you are playing a DANGEROUS game, a game where many have been totally wiped out. The markets are far more volatile than we think with a lot of surprise volatility. You need to buy some cheap puts or calls to offset your naked exposure. You do this by buying much cheaper out-of-the-money options and creating a credit spread. For example, if you sell (write) a Dow Chemical April 10 put at 1, you could buy an April 5 put for .2. Now you have a credit of .8 instead of 1, but have limited your risk to 4.2(5 − .8 = 4.2).

Let's look at another example in a different way. Whenever you write an option, you receive credit into your account. If you sell an IBM April 90 call for 3, you receive $300 into your account. To offset the risk of writing (selling) this option, you buy IBM APR 95 for 1. Now you have reduced your credit to $200 (3 − 1 = 2). This is a credit spread. The most you can lose is $300 because you stop losing money if IBM is above 95 (90 − 95 = 5 less 2 = 3). (Again, it is important to emphasize that you should always use stop-loss orders to get you out of positions when stop losses are hit.)

Spreads are classified as either debit or credit spreads, depending on whether they initially put money into your account, which is a credit to your account, or take money out of your account, which is a debit to your account. Credit spreads are usually writing strategies. They are a way to write a naked option with limited risk. On the other hand, debit spreads are usually buying strategies where you, in a sense, buy options at discount prices, also with limited risk.

AN INDEX OR ETF CREDIT SPREAD

As previously mentioned, writing naked index options theoretically seems like a powerful strategy, but that strategy backfired for many during the 1987 crash when they discovered what unlimited risk really means. There is a way to neutralize most of that risk and prevent the devastating losses that occurred in 1987. The answer is an *index credit* spread.

You write (sell) one index option, and to reduce the risk of a naked writer, you buy a cheaper, further out-of-the-money option with the same expiration date. For example, if you write the S&P 100 Index (OEX) July 380 call for 1.5, you may then buy the 385 call for .5. Therefore, you would receive in your account a credit of $100, less commissions (1.5 − .5 = 1[$100]).

You have an option writing position, so if the S&P 100 Index does not move above 380 before expiration, both the 380 and 385 calls will expire and you will pocket the $100. However, if the S&P 100 Index moves against you, the most you can lose is $400. Why? You have added a new, more important line of defense. By purchasing the 385 call, you stop losing money if the OEX moves above 385 because the 385 call will increase in value at the same rate as the 380 call you have written. Therefore, the most that you can lose is the difference between the strike price of the call you are writing and the call you are buying (385 − 380 = 5), or $500 less your credit of $100, giving you a maximum loss of $400. This is naked writing with limited risk.

With credit spreading, you have limited risk, but your risk can be high if the difference between the option that your write and buy is large, or if you write a lot of options. For example, a 15 point spread involves a possible loss of $1,500. If you do ten of the spreads, your possible loss is $15,000.

THE TRACK RECORD

Between December of 1988 and June of 1991, I recommended twenty-seven index credit spreads in my newsletter, *The Trester Complete Option Report*. The theoretical results of these spreads showed that two were losers and twenty-five were profitable. In other words, over 90% were profitable. If you had entered ten contracts on each credit spread, your net profit would have been $10,518, after subtracting deep discount commissions of $1,920. The average margin requirement per position would have been $9,365, and the profit per position would be $389.

Between June of 1988 and June of 1991, thirty-six similar index credit spreads were recommended in my other newsletter, *The Put and Call Tactician*. The theoretical portfolio shows that thirty-two, or 89%, were profitable. The recommended position size ranged from five to ten contracts. The average margin required for each position was $7,875. The net profit for all positions was $16,186, less commissions of $2,460, giving a net profit of $13,726. Almost all positions were held for less than one month, and twelve out of thirty-six were held for less than one or two weeks. Therefore, the annualized return would have been over 70%.

In addition to the track record results, many students who have taken my investment seminars and college classes have had great success with this strategy over all other option plays.

GUIDELINES FOR DEVELOPING INDEX CREDIT SPREADS

Here are the guidelines for developing an index credit spread as described in the track record above.

1. Only write overpriced index options on broad-based indexes, such as the S&P 500 Index or the ETF (SPY).

2. Only write options that are far out-of-the-money. The key to success in designing such a spread is to write an index option where the index price is far from the strike price. Then the chance is small that you will ever take a loss. This action is another line of defense against risk.

3. Set a stop-loss that is out-of-the-money. Make sure to close out the whole spread before the index price can cause a lot of damage to your spread. With such a stop-loss, rarely if ever will you incur the maximum loss.

4. Never enter a credit spread where the credit is less than .35. A credit of .25 or .3 is too small reward for a potential risk of 5, 10 or 15 points, especially after commissions.

5. Try to stay with 5 or 10-point spreads (the difference between the option you are writing and buying). Don't go beyond a 15-point spread.

6. Only write index spreads that have one month or less before expiration. Maximum depreciation occurs in the last month, and with less time you have a higher probability of profit.

7. Only use spread orders to enter and exit such spreads.

8. Only use deep discount brokers and do at least five options at a time to reduce the commission cost per option. Such spreads require two and sometimes four commissions. Don't let them eat up your profits.

9. Avoid bucking the market trend. If the market is in a strong up trend, only enter put credit

spreads. If the market is in a major decline, only enter call credit spreads. When the market moves against you, cover your position even if the stop-loss has not been touched. This is another line of defense.

How can you tell if you have designed a good credit spread? *Option Master*, a computer program, tells you your probability of profit or the tables at the back of this book can help. If it is 85% or higher and if you followed the guidelines just presented, you have a theoretically profitable spread.

The reward from such credit spreading may seem small, but because you win almost all of the time, the annualized return is quite high.

And the Best Sure Bet Play Is . . .

The winner for the best Sure Bet Play is option writing with which you can win 90% of the time. Here is the Writing Option Strategy in capsule form.

THE THREE MAIN WAYS TO WRITE (SELL) OPTIONS

First, to buy or sell stocks, always write options. If you buy stocks, you should be writing puts.

Second, if you are a high risk player, you can write naked puts and calls, but this method is not advised unless you are very diversified or are dealing with low priced stocks and are writing puts.

Finally, if you do not want to buy stocks and want limited risk, write credit spreads.

THE NECESSARY STEPS YOU MUST TAKE

1. *Scientifically Determine the Probability of Profit*

   To develop a high probability strategy by writing options, you first must develop a probability of profit, and that is not a random guess on your part. You need to follow a more scientific method. With horse racing you had a very long history of statistics to work with. With options you are able to use computer simulation to measure the chances of profiting.

   The key ingredient in the simulations is the volatility (how much the underlying stock or fund price moves up and down over a set time period). Predicting short-term stock or fund price moves is very difficult if not impossible, but predicting stock or fund or commodity volatility is much easier. When stock prices are volatile, they stay volatile for a while. When stock prices are quiet or less volatile, they stay that way for a while. When volatility numbers are stable, you will get accurate results from your computer simulations.

   There are several computer programs that can run computer simulations. One of those programs is *Option Master Deluxe* (GoOptions.com). Such a program will give you the probability of making a profit with an option writing strategy.

To be successful, the option you are writing must be far out-of-the-money. In other words, the strike price of the option must be away from the stock or index price. In addition, there should be a short time before the option will expire, usually a month or a month and a half or less. If you are writing a call option under these circumstances, the stock price can go down, go down a lot, stay where it is or go up a small amount, and you will win. The computer simulation will then show a high probability of profit.

Try to select strategies where the probability of profit is 85% or better. Also, the simulations should assume a random market. Furthermore, make sure you have a stop-loss in place based on the underlying stock or ETF price.

2. *Find Overpriced Options for a Statistical Advantage*

Now that you have a high probability of profit, you need to gain a statistical advantage regarding the option price. Try to select overpriced options. Our *Option Master Pro* (formally 2000) can scan all stock and ETF options and pick the most overpriced options based on your criteria.

3. *Go for Short Term Profits*

Finally make your option strategy as short term as possible, one or two months or less. Also, be aggressive about taking profits. When the option you have written loses most of its value, take profits!

4. *Use Credit Spreads*

A reminder that the best way to play our Sure Bet writing strategy is to do credit spreads. Remember, in a bear market on market rallies, do call credit spreads, and in a bull market when the market declines do put credit spreads.

5. *Exit When Necessary*

Defense is critical. Avoid getting in the way of a strong move in the market. When you are uncomfortable in a position, get out.

6. *Diversify!*

Finally, diversify; do not take large positions. Then if you do get hit with a loss, it will not be a large one.

Now WE HAVE MET ALL THE REQUIRE-MENTS OR OBJECTIVES OF A SURE BET STRATEGY: HIGH PROBABILITY, PROFITABIL-ITY AND A SHORT TIME FRAME. Yet there is even one more advantage to writing options.

7. *Buy Stock at a Discount*

Option writing is not only a way of getting to our Sure Bet investment strategy, but, as you know, also a way to buy stocks or ETFs at a discount or get paid for waiting to sell a stock at your price. Here is another example of how this works. If FX is at $80 a share and you want to buy 100 shares at $60 a share, you can write a $60 put. If the put is selling at 2, you receive $200 into your account. If FX is below 60 at expiration, you get the 100 shares of stock and keep the $200. As a result, your cost is $58 a share.

Now if you own 100 shares of FX and wanted to sell it at $90 a share, you could write a 90 call for 2 ($200). If the stock is above 90 at expiration, you would have sold the stock at 90 plus have $200 as a bonus. In both cases if you don't buy the stock or sell the stock, you keep the $200 as a consolation prize.

OUR TRACK RECORD

Finally, we should emphasize, again, the importance of our track record. We have been recommending high probability option writing strategies in our *Option Report* newsletter since 1982, and every year these strategies pay off and generate a theoretical profit for the year. That is a long track record and proves that the science and mathematics behind these strategies is correct. Use the strategies, take the precautions, do your homework and you are very close to a sure thing. The odds are that you'll be a winner.

Do You Have a Good or Bad Play?

18

Let's Do It!

Now that we have the guidelines to follow, *Let's Do It!* First, you need to open a brokerage account and get approved to trade options. Second, you have to have the necessary trading knowledge, and reading this book gives you that trading knowledge. (If, however, you want more, read *The Complete Option Player*, a very easy-to-understand book.)

Next, you may need a computer program that does simulations, for you need to know your odds. Three programs that will do the simulations are: *Option Master Deluxe*, *The Push-Button Option Writer* and *The Push-Button Spread Trader*, available at GoOptions.com. Or you can use the tables at the back of this book.

Now the tough part is picking the stock, ETF, or commodity. In the stock market you now can play almost anything with ETFs. That includes metals like gold and silver, currencies like the yen or the euro, bonds like the treasuries or high yield funds, and energy complex such as crude oil. Besides, you can go short, double or triple short or long for these entities.

Next, if you don't mind owning 100 shares of the underlying stock or ETF, you can write naked puts. If you don't mind selling 100 shares of stock you own, you can write covered calls.

To apply our Sure Bet Strategy, you should have an 85% or better chance of profiting by having the option expire. With the *Push-Button Option Writer* (PBOW), this is easy. For a stock you wish to buy, just enter the stock price. The PBOW will recommend an option for you to write. However, you can enter another option if you wish. Then just click on Generate Profit Box, and the program will give you the probability of profit and will rate the position. Make sure the probability of profit is less than 15%. That means there is a 85% chance the option will expire, which is what you want. Try to find plays that have a rating of 100 or better.

A GOOD OR BAD PLAY?

The beauty of the PBOW is that it will tell you if you have a good or a bad play. A rating above 100 is a good play. A rating below 80 is a bad play. Also, a good play is one where you have a 80% or better chance of the option expiring without hitting your stop-loss price, in which case you are the winner. Although if you really want the stock, you are a winner under both circumstances.

A WEAPON FOR THE WALL STREET WARS

If you don't have a computer program, you can use the High Price Tables at the back of this book to guide you in determining the probability of profits. The *High Price Call and Put Tables* tell you the likely high price on average that an option will reach, and they also tell you the probability of hitting that price.

Try to write options that show a probability of 20% or less; that means you will win 80% of the time! Average volatility is about 30%, and high volatility is over 40%. Check the *Volatility Measurement Table*. These tools will provide estimates, but the computer programs do a much more exact job.

IDENTIFYING OVERVALUED OPTIONS

All the programs we have mentioned will tell you whether the option is over or undervalued. The PBOW and *Push-Button Spread Trader* (PBST) will give you the implied volatility of the option. That helps tell you if the option is over or undervalued. If the implied

The Volatility Measurement Table

		The Common Stock's High Price																	
	$5	10	15	20	25	30	35	40	45	50	55	60	65	70	75	80	85	90	95
$5	0%	66%	99%	99%	99%	99%	99%	99%	99%	99%	99%	99%	99%	99%	99%	99%	99%	99%	99%
10		0%	40%	66%	85%	99%	99%	99%	99%	99%	99%	99%	99%	99%	99%	99%	99%	99%	99%
15			0%	28%	50%	66%	80%	90%	99%	99%	99%	99%	99%	99%	99%	99%	99%	99%	99%
20				0%	22%	40%	54%	66%	76%	85%	93%	99%	99%	99%	99%	99%	99%	99%	99%
25					0%	18%	33%	46%	57%	66%	75%	82%	88%	94%	99%	99%	99%	99%	99%
30						0%	15%	28%	40%	50%	58%	66%	73%	80%	85%	90%	95%	99%	99%
35							0%	13%	25%	35%	44%	52%	60%	66%	72%	78%	83%	88%	92%
40								0%	11%	22%	31%	40%	47%	54%	60%	66%	72%	76%	81%
45									0%	10%	20%	28%	36%	43%	50%	56%	61%	66%	71%
50										0%	9. %	18%	26%	33%	40%	46%	51%	57%	62%
55											0%	8. %	16%	24%	30%	37%	42%	48%	53%
60												0%	8%	15%	22%	28%	34%	40%	45%
65													0%	7. %	14%	20%	26%	32%	37%
70														0%	6. %	13%	19%	25%	30%
75															0%	6. %	12%	18%	23%
80																0%	6. %	11%	17%
85																	0%	5. %	11%
90																		0%	5. %
95																			0%

The Common Stock's Low Price

Volatility levels which show 99%, represent volatility levels which are over 100%. Refer to Figure I to determine the exact volatility percentage.

volatility is over 50%, the option is usually overvalued. If the implied volatility is under 25, the option is usually undervalued. *Option Master Deluxe* gives you a more exact measure of fair value. Also, many of the internet brokers provide tools for measuring whether an option is over or underpriced. If you don't have a computer, *The Complete Option Player* book has tables that help you measure fair value.

Let's look at an example. Let us say that you would not mind owning 100 shares of Petroleum Brasileiro, the big oil company from Brazil, at a price of 37 with its current price of 41.9. Here you could sell (write) the Mar 37 put at .5. What is your chance of hitting your stop-loss? We will set that point at 37. Using the PBOW simulator, we get 17%. So, there is an 83% chance that the option will expire, using a volatility of 30%, about average for most stocks. Check the Option Profit Box Downside Worksheet, Table 1. The rating is 103, which is over 100, so this is a good play.

Now let's try an ETF option of the Gold Trust (GLD), in other words, gold in the form of gold futures. On February 2, 2010, GLD was 109.2. If we write the SPDR Gold Trust Mar 99 put, there is only a 15% chance of hitting the 98.5 stop-loss, but the rating was only 76, a bad play! Why? You have too much exposure if the stop-loss is hit, unless you want to buy the gold stock. Then you have an 85% winner. Check Table 2.

DESIGNING SPREADS

If you don't want to buy stock or sell stock but wish to do option writing, you should design a credit spread, unless you are writing puts on very low-priced stocks.

To design a spread, you can use the PBST.

1. Enter the stock price.

2. Enter an option to write.

3. Enter the option price.

Then find a further out-of-the-money option that is really cheap to buy and enter that into the program.

To find a really cheap option to buy, you may need to work with shorter term options that expire in two months or less. The difference between the option you are writing and the option you are buying is your credit. That credit should be .35 or better.

BAILOUT POINTS

With any credit spread, you should set a stop-loss price based on the underlying stock or ETF price. As you know, the stop-loss price is a price where you will automatically exit the position if the price is hit. Try to set your stop-loss at or slightly out-of-the-money. If it is in-the-money, set it very close to the strike price. Never allow your position to move deep in-the-money. Try to

TABLE 1—The Push Button Option Writer

OPTION PROFIT BOX®
Downside Worksheet
02-02-2010

** OPENING ACTION **
1. Sell Petroleo Brasileiro (PBR) Mar 37-PUT Options at 0.5 (Stock Priced at 41.9)
2. After entry, buy back the options if the stock hits the stop-loss of 36.5

** SURVEILLANCE ACTION **
3. Once in the position, plot the closing price of the underlying common stock
   in the Option Profit Box® below:

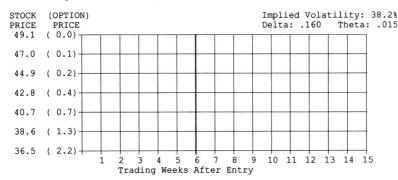

STOCK PRICE	(OPTION) PRICE	
49.1	(0.0)	
47.0	(0.1)	
44.9	(0.2)	
42.8	(0.4)	
40.7	(0.7)	
38.6	(1.3)	
36.5	(2.2)	

Implied Volatility: 38.2%
Delta: .160   Theta: .015

Trading Weeks After Entry

Prob of Downside Exit: 19%   Expected Value: $7.6
Annualized Return: 548.2%   Rating: 103

** CLOSING ACTION **
After you enter an Option Profit Box®, one of two possibilities can occur.
The plot of the underlying common stock can exit the Box at the RIGHT SIDE
or BOTTOM. Your action and the end result of the trade is detailed
here:

4. RIGHT SIDE Exit - The time has expired in the trade.
5. BOTTOM Exit - This requires stop-loss action on your part. BUY BACK
   the options at the market price.

** RECORD OF TRANSACTION **

	Date	Quantity	Price	Dollars (Net)	
Opening					
Closing					
					Profit (Loss)

TABLE 2—The Push Button Option Writer

OPTION PROFIT BOX®
Downside Worksheet

02-02-2010

** OPENING ACTION **
1. Sell SPDR GOLD TRUST Mar 99-PUT Options at 0.5 (Stock Priced at 109.2)
2. After entry, buy back the options if the stock hits the stop-loss of 98.5

** SURVEILLANCE ACTION **
3. Once in the position, plot the closing price of the underlying common stock
   in the Option Profit Box® below:

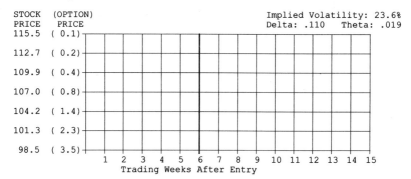

```
STOCK   (OPTION)                          Implied Volatility: 23.6%
PRICE    PRICE                            Delta: .110    Theta: .019
115.5   ( 0.1)
112.7   ( 0.2)
109.9   ( 0.4)
107.0   ( 0.8)
104.2   ( 1.4)
101.3   ( 2.3)
 98.5   ( 3.5)
         1  2  3  4  5  6  7  8  9  10 11 12 13 14 15
              Trading Weeks After Entry
```

Prob of Downside Exit: 15%   Expected Value: ($2.8)
Annualized Return: 401.1%   Rating: 76

** CLOSING ACTION **
After you enter an Option Profit Box®, one of two possibilities can occur.
The plot of the underlying common stock can exit the Box at the RIGHT SIDE
or BOTTOM. Your action and the end result of the trade is detailed
here:

4. RIGHT SIDE Exit - The time has expired in the trade.
5. BOTTOM Exit - This requires stop-loss action on your part. BUY BACK
   the options at the market price.

** RECORD OF TRANSACTION **

	Date	Quantity	Price	Dollars (Net)
Opening				
Closing				
				Profit (Loss)

TABLE 3—The Push Button Spread Trader

OPTION PROFIT BOX®   01-31-2010

** OPENING ACTION **
1. Buy PRUDENTIAL Feb 55-CALL Options at 0.5. Sell Feb 60-CALL Options at 0.1.

** SURVEILLANCE ACTION **
2. Once in the position, daily plot the closing price of the underlying
   common stock in the Option Profit Box® below:

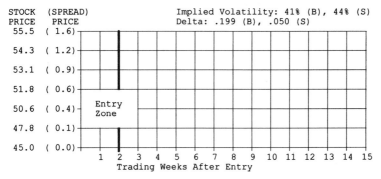

STOCK PRICE	(SPREAD) PRICE	Implied Volatility: 41% (B), 44% (S) Delta: .199 (B), .050 (S)
55.5	(1.6)	
54.3	(1.2)	
53.1	(0.9)	
51.8	(0.6)	
50.6	(0.4)	Entry Zone
47.8	(0.1)	
45.0	(0.0)	

1 2 3 4 5 6 7 8 9 10 11 12 13 14 15
Trading Weeks After Entry

Prob of Upside Exit: 15%   Expected Value: ($10.9)
Prob of Downside Exit: 8%   Rating: Good (3)

** CLOSING ACTION **
After you enter an Option Profit Box®, one of three possibilities can occur.
The daily plot of the underlying common stock can exit the Box at the TOP,
RIGHT SIDE, or BOTTOM. Exit your position if the stock leaves the box.

** RECORD OF TRANSACTION **

	Date	Quantity	Price	Dollars (Net)
Opening				
Closing				
				Profit (Loss)

design credit spreads that have a 5 point spread or less, such as a 2.5 points spread. Remember, the size of the spread is your maximum risk. A 5 point spread has $500 of risk; a 2.5 spread has $250 of risk.

Using the simulator in the *Push-Button Spread Trader* (PBST), let's look at a Prudential (PRU) example. With PRU priced at 50.6, we will sell (write) the Feb 55 call at .5 ($50) on Jan 31. To offset the risk of this play, we will buy the Feb 60 call at .1 ($10), and we will set a stop-loss of 55.5. The simulator says there is a 15% chance that the stock will hit 55.5 before expiration on Feb 19, so there is an 85% chance of winning. The PBST rates the strategy as "Good". Check Table 3.

TRUE CONFESSIONS

Many students have asked me, what do I play? First, 80% of my plays since 1973 have been option writing plays. Most of the option writing plays are naked puts where I don't mind owning the stock. Sometimes I write pure naked puts and calls and do not want the stock, but I don't recommend this strategy to anyone else. I do credit spreads, but not as many as most would think. To protect against risk, I *diversify, diversify, diversify* and only take very small positions. Since 1973 from my own account I have made a profit every year writing options. I have never been hit by a bad loss even during the crash of 1987. However, I am paranoid about closing positions that start to go bad. I also only do high probability plays.

What I love about option writing is that I win almost all the time. There is not another game where you can do that!

Reward— Conclusion

Hopefully, the illusion of a sure bet has been replaced by the reality of just how close you can get to that goal. True, you have to understand what you're up against:

Efficient markets that are almost impossible to predict,

A smart crowd to compete with,

False gurus and systems that tempt you,

Lady Luck who deceives you,

The random nature of the market (life as well),

The rogue waves that can topple your world,

And journalists and financial analysts who bombard you with false information.

Despite these obstacles, the investor still has a chance to be a winner. At the race track, in the stock market and on the options floor, we have found the strategies, backed up by science and mathematics, that can get you close to the sure thing; the reward for your journey from illusion to reality.

APPENDIX

Tutorial

What is the option game? It's an investment strategy that involves paying for the right to buy or sell stock or futures at a particular price over a given time, or selling the right to someone else to buy or sell stock or futures for a particular price over a given time. Simple? Actually, yes.

However, there is a bit of *pretending* going on. Most of the investors only *pretend* to want to buy or sell the stock they control. What they are really doing in this game is betting a particular stock or futures *price* will go up or go down.

That bet is called an *option,* and the casino palaces are *options exchanges,* the first constructed in the early 1970's. You can play the part of the tourist or the casino owner. Want to play?

Before you can learn the tricks of the trade, you have to know the game, and that is what this section is all about, teaching you the basics of option trading. (The good stuff comes later.) Let's begin.

Throughout the tutorial, we will use stocks to explain option trading, but keep in mind that what applies to stock and stock options applies to futures and futures options.

THE LISTED OPTION

The first step in becoming an effective option player is to gain a complete understanding of the focal point of the game—the *listed option.* A listed option is a stock option (remember, think futures, too), and an option is simply a contract, one that gives you the right to buy or sell 100 shares of stock at a specific price for a specific period of time. While stock options have been with us for a long time, the brilliant idea of creating a *listed* option opened up a whole new investment medium.

As a result, listed options are stock options that are liquid, standardized and continually created at the changing price levels of the common stock. When we say a listed option is *liquid,* we mean that it can be bought and sold at any time in an auction market similar to the New York Stock Exchange.

Formerly in the old over-the-counter (OTC) market, if you could find a seller, stock options could be purchased, but in order to have taken your profits from that option, you would have had to exercise the option, actually buying the 100 shares of the stock that you had the right to purchase. Now with the options exchanges this costly process of actually buying the stock or selling the stock is not necessary. All you have to do is go back to the Exchange and sell your option.

THE LISTED CALL AND PUT

There are two types of listed options: the listed *call* option that gives you the right to buy stock and the listed *put* option that gives you the right to sell stock. When you purchase a *call*, you are betting that the underlying stock price will move up. When you purchase a *put*, you are betting that the underlying stock price will move down.

PARTS OF THE WHOLE, THE LISTED OPTION

Using stock options, a listed option has four major segments:

I. The RIGHT—to buy or sell 100 shares of a specific stock

II. The EXPIRATION DATE—the date that your right ends or expires

III. The STRIKE PRICE—the price at which you can buy or sell

IV. The OPTION PRICE—the price you paid for the right to buy or sell 100 shares at an exercise (strike) price until an expiration date

This is an example of a listed call option:

IBM Jul 60 (at) 3

Let's look at each part.

Part I: "IBM"—This represents the stock name. This option is the right to buy 100 shares of IBM Corporation common stock.

Part II: "Jul"—This represents the time when your right expires. This is the *expiration date* which falls on the Saturday immediately following the third Friday of the expiration month. In this case, it is the month of July.

Part III: "60"—This represents the exercise price at which the IBM stock can be purchased. This price is also referred to as the *strike* price."

Part IV: "(at) 3"—This refers to the last transaction price at which this option was bought or sold with one qualifying point. The 3 represents $3, the price to buy one share of stock. All listed options carry the right to buy or sell 100 shares of stock. Therefore, always multiply the price by 100 to get the true price of the option. In this case, the true price is $300. ($3 × 100 = $300).

THE OPTIONS EXCHANGE

The venues for trading listed options are called the *options exchanges*. An options exchange, like a stock exchange, is an auction market where buyers and sellers gather to trade securities; in this case, the securities are listed options. The first of these exchanges, the Chicago Board Options Exchange (CBOE), was established in April of 1973. Because of its success, others have been established. They are our *casino palaces*.

(Again, remember when we say "stocks," we also are referring to futures.)

Options are also available on stock market indexes, such as the Dow Jones Industrial Average, S&P 500 Index and the S&P 100 Index, which includes 100 large capitalized stocks in its average.

The stocks that are listed on the option exchanges must meet a set of strict criteria.

Each individual stock must have at least three different options listed on the Exchange but can have many more. Each common stock has listed options that expire in the next two months, and every three months—up to nine months in the future.

In addition, in 1990, long term options were introduced. The long term options can run more than two years before they expire and are referred to as Leaps® (Long-Term Equity Anticipation Securities).

Why do some stocks have more options and more strike prices than others? When options for a stock are first listed on the Exchange, options with one or two strike prices will become available. According to the rules, each will have four to eight listed options for a specific stock. If there is a significant change in the market price of the underlying common stock, new options with new strike prices then become available. Normally, options with new strike prices are established at 5-point intervals, unless the stock is below 50. Then strike prices are usually available at 2-1/2-point intervals. Many stocks have hundreds of different options available.

THE PRICE OF AN OPTION

The price is the most important element of a listed option. The price of an option is set on the Options Exchange according to two different values: *intrinsic* and *time value.*

Intrinsic Value

The *intrinsic value* is the *real* value of the option. This means that if you exercise your call option contract (which you normally never do in the options market), you will purchase 100 shares of the common stock at a lower price than the current market price of the common stock. Thus, the option has some real value.

If you were to exercise a put option contract with intrinsic value, you would sell 100 shares of stock at a higher price than the current market value of the common stock—the put option would then have real value.

Time Value

Remember that an option is a right you have for a period of time. You must pay for that right, and the amount of money you must pay is referred to as *time value*, which is what the market thinks the intrinsic value of an option will be in the future.

As time passes, the value of an option will decrease. In fact, the time value of an option continually declines to "0" as time passes and the option reaches the end of its life.

The time value is the most important factor that we work with. In many cases, the options you buy will be options with time value only—no intrinsic value.

Intrinsic Value + Time Value = Option Price

Here two concepts should be explained: *in-the-money* and *out-of-the-money*. A call option is *in-the-money* when the *strike price*, the price at which you can buy the stock, is lower than the current market price. *Out-of-the-money* is, of course, the opposite; the strike price is higher than the current market price.

The option will probably be cheaper to buy when it is out-of-the-money, but buying the option, you are hoping that time will cure this and bring you in-the-money before your time (the option) is up.

An experienced player, whether he is a buyer or a writer (the seller of the option, the role of the casino owner), will spend most of his time with *out-of-the-money* options—options that only have time value.

To summarize, the option price is determined by adding intrinsic value to time value. Intrinsic value is the real value of the option. The time value is the value that you place on the possibility that the option will attain some intrinsic value by having the stock price move through the strike price and into-the-money.

Volatility

An obvious truth—to achieve success in betting a stock will move up or down, you have to bet on stocks that are known to move up or down. Therefore, another element that controls the price of a listed option is the *price volatility* of the underlying common stock, the amount that the stock price moves up and down.

A common stock price that has high volatility normally moves in very wide ranges over a period of time. A volatile stock may move from 40% to 60% off its base price annually. Such wide price movements give it a much greater probability of moving through the strike price of a listed option, and, as a result, that option will take on more premium (time value).

On the other hand, a stock with low volatility normally trades within a narrow range, not moving very far in any one direction. This will have a negative effect on the option price because the probability of the stock price moving through the strike price is diminished.

However, understanding stock volatility in the options market can be tricky. In some cases, a common stock that has been historically quite volatile may reach periods in which it is somewhat dormant, and, conversely, stocks that are normally quite low in price volatility will suddenly move dramatically in one direction or another. These shifts in price behavior will alter the influence of this factor on the listed option.

Liquidity

Though the price of the underlying stock, the time left in the life of an option, and the volatility of the underlying stock can be factors that constitute 90% of the price of the stock option, another factor that has a powerful indirect influence on option price behavior is the amount of *liquidity* that exists in a specific listed option. Liquidity refers to trading volume, or the ability to move in and out of an option position easily.

Liquidity requires that plenty of buyers and sellers be available to ensure such transactions. Options that do not have liquidity may trap you into a position or prevent you from taking a large enough position to make the transaction worthwhile. Liquidity in the options market can be measured by the number of specific listed options that are traded every day and the open interest; open interest means the number of contracts that have not been closed out and are presently open.

For example, how many IBM Jul 60 calls are traded on the average day? Calculating this average would give you an idea of this option's liquidity. Note that liquidity changes throughout the life of a specific option. The IBM Jul 60 call may have no liquidity at all when the stock is at 90 because the option is so far *in-the-money* that no one is interested in that option. On the other hand, it may not have any liquidity at all if the stock is at 30 because now the option is so far *out-of-the-money* that it hardly has any value at all.

Also, if there are eight months left in that IBM Jul 60 call, its price may be so high that it will lack the necessary liquidity to be an effective trading vehicle. In fact, options that usually have lives of seven, eight, or nine months normally do not have the liquidity that an option of two or three months would maintain.

OPTION WRITERS

If you are buying the right to sell or buy stock at a certain price over a given time, you have to be buying that right from someone. That *someone* is the *option writer*. In other words, if option buying is analogous to a side bet on the price action of a specific stock, the backer of that side bet is the option writer, the casino owner.

He takes the bets of the option buyer and, in a sense, pays off when the option buyer is a winner. When the option buyer is the loser, he pockets the option proceeds, what the buyer paid for the option.

Put simply, option writers sell an option rather than buy it. The option seller (writer) has a time advantage over the option buyer because unlike the buyer, *time* works for the seller. As time passes, the value of the option depreciates. This depreciation, this value, slips into the pocket of the option writer.

Let's take an example. Let's say that you purchase a call option—an Intel October 25 call. Let's say that there are three months left in the life of that option, and you pay a price of $300, plus commissions. At the same time that you are buying that option, someone unknown to you, on the other side of the Options Exchange is selling (writing) that option and is receiving your $300.

This money will go into his account, so, in a sense,

you have just put $300 into the pocket of the option writer. Now he has certain obligations. If you request 100 shares of Intel by exercising your option, he must deliver to you 100 shares of Intel stock at a price of 25.

Let's assume that the Intel price is now at 23, which means we are working with an *out-of-the-money* option. One month passes, and the stock has moved from 23 to 24. The Intel Oct 25 has depreciated in value from $300 to $200, even though the stock has moved upward.

The option writer now has a paper profit of $100, less commissions. If he wishes, he can go back into the Options Exchange, buy that option back for $200, take his profits and, in a sense, close the casino door.

On the other hand, if he thinks that Intel is going to stay where it is or not move any further than 26 or 27 on the upside, he can hang onto that option and wait for it to continue to depreciate to zero. If you, the option buyer, hold onto the option, you will continue to see it depreciate in value, unless the stock moves up suddenly in a strong and positive direction.

In other words, the option writer has an advantage. While he is backing your bet, or option, it is depreciating. You, the option buyer, while holding that bet are losing money. However, if you prefer, you can be the option writer rather than the buyer.

That's right. You, too, can be an option writer. You

can take the role of the casino or bookie. Where else can you do this legally?

Two Types of Option Writers

The *covered option writer* and the *uncovered* (*naked*) *writer* are the two types of option writers.

The *covered option writer* sells an option on 100 shares of stock that he has bought (owns). He benefits from selling the option, having the time value of the option on his side and, at the same time, profits from the upward move of the stock, offsetting any possible losses from the option he has just written. This kind of strategy is very conservative and the most popular today.

The *uncovered* (*naked*) *writer*, on the other hand, is very speculative and writes (sells) the option on 100 shares of stock that he does not own. There is unlimited risk to the naked *call* writer (betting the stock won't go up) and extensive risk to the naked *put* writer (betting the stock won't go down).

To guarantee to both the options buyer and to the Options Exchange that the naked writer will make good on the options that he writes, he must put up cash and/or collateral to back up his naked option writing position.

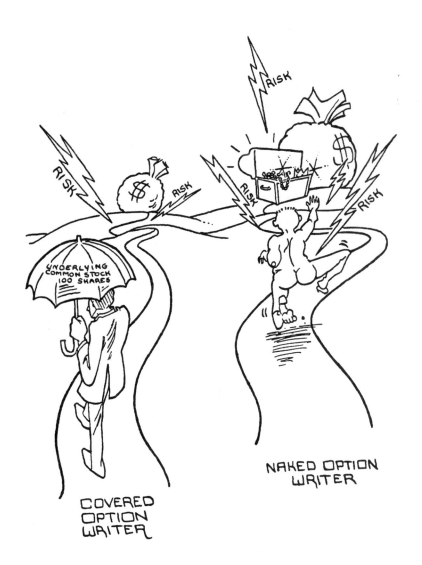

COVERED
OPTION
WRITER

NAKED OPTION
WRITER

The How-to to Option Writing

The only difference between buying and writing options lies in the order in which you carry out the process. The option writer sells an option to open a position and buys an option to close that position. This process releases him from the responsibilities that are part of his option obligations. Conversely, the option buyer buys an option to open a position and sells an option to close the position, an act that relinquishes the rights that he purchased with that option.

The option writer, like the option buyer in the options market, has the advantage of liquidity. At one moment, he can write an option, and at the next moment, he can close out that position on the Exchange by buying back the option. In this way, the shrewd option writer can avoid being assigned (exercised) by the option buyer or exposing himself to the potential dangers of option writing.

Exercise Defined

Here is where *exercise* should be more thoroughly explained. When you buy an option, whether it is a put or a call, you are buying a right to exercise. When we say *exercise* with regard to a call option, we mean to *call* from the writer (seller/backer) of the option the 100 shares of stock as specified in the option at the specified option strike price. The writer is required to deliver that

100 shares of the stock at specified strike price to the buyer if the option is exercised by the buyer.

With regard to a put option, we mean to *put* (sell) to the writer of the option the 100 shares of stock as specified in the option at the specified option strike price. The writer is required to buy that 100 shares of stock at the specified strike price from the option buyer if the option is exercised by the buyer. The writer who is being exercised is being *assigned* the obligation to deliver or buy the stock randomly by the Options Clearing Corporation. Therefore, the process of exercise is called *assignment.*

SPREAD DESIGNER

The Debit Spread

The *debit spread* is a way to buy an option at a lower price. The disadvantage is that you limit your profits. To design a limited risk debit spread, follow these steps:

1. Select an option you wish to buy, i.e. IBM Jan 70 call at 3.
2. Select an option you wish to sell in the same month but make sure it is out-of-the-money by 2.5, 5, 10 or more points, i.e. IBM Jan 75 call at 1.
3. Subtract the price of the option you have sold from the option you have bought, i.e. Jan 75 call

at 1 from Jan 70 call at 3, and your total cost would be 2.

4. The result is the cost of the spread and your maximum risk.

5. The maximum gain can be measured by subtracting the cost of the spread from the maximum possible gain (which is the difference between the strike prices of the spread; i.e. 70–75 is a 5 point spread.) Using the IBM example, you will see that 75–70 is the spread, and the cost of the spread is 2, so the maximum gain is 3.

6. To evaluate a spread, you need to look at the maximum possible percent return and the probability of making a profit and making the maximum return. In our example, the maximum return for the IBM 70–75 spread would be 150% (300/200 = 150%). A probability calculator can be used to measure your probability of achieving such returns. With the IBM spread, IBM must close above 75 at expiration to achieve a maximum return.

The Credit Spread

The *credit spread* can be a way to write options with limited risk. There are two types of credit spreads, but all of them put cash or a credit in your account.

To design a basic credit spread, do and understand the following:

1. Select an option you wish to write, i.e. PFE Jan 40 call at 2.
2. Select an option further out-of-the-money to buy, i.e. PFE Jan 45 call at 1.
3. The difference between the two prices is the credit that you receive, i.e. 2 – 1=1; credit of 1.
4. Your maximum risk is the difference between the strike prices, i.e. 45 – 40=5; maximum risk is 5 points, less the credit you receive; 5 – 1=4 points is your maximum risk.

Onward!

You now know the jargon and basics of option trading. If you keep the basics in mind, they will be a foundation for option trading success. How to build on that foundation, choosing between a myriad of trading strategies and tactics and picking those that suit your goals and personality, comes next. In this book the secrets of option trading will be revealed, and you will have in your hands the tools to build your dreams.

The High Price Tables

The High Price Tables were created by computer simulation for the use of option buyers and naked option writers. These tables are special tactical tools that will aid you in;

Measuring the potential risk and return from a strategy.

Designing a game plan to determine the optimum point in time to take profits.

Designing safeguards for naked writing strategies such as setting bail-out points.

Providing a better picture of the future behavior of the option price.

These are just a few the ways the High Price Tables can be used in the options game. You will discover others as you use the tables

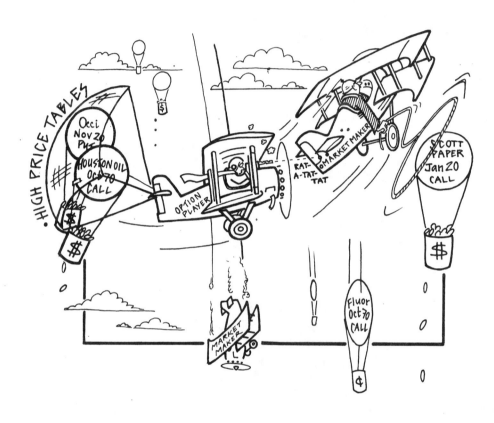

HOW TO USE THE HIGH PRICE TABLES

The High Price Tables provide two valuable pieces of information on each option, both puts and calls. First, through our computer simulations they disclose the average high price that an option will reach before it expires.

AVERAGE HIGH PRICE is determined by simulating the stock and corresponding option price action thousands of times. Then from each trial simulation, the high option price reached during the life of the option is included in determining the average high price for all the simulated trials. Each individual strategy may not reach the average high price because it is an average. The chances of reaching that high price are presented just below the average high price figure in the tables.

Second, the tables display the percentage probability that the option will reach or move above that average high price before it expires.

For example, using the High Price Call Tables, the ABC July 50 call with 3 months until expiration, we can find the *average high price* that the option is likely to reach in the next three months before it expires.

Looking under the *High* volatility category, we find the average high price based on our high price, based on our computer simulations, is 5.3 when the ABC stock price is 48.

Just below the high price of 5.3, we find the percentage chance that the option price will actually reach or go beyond the high price. . In the example, the ABC July 50 call has a 40% chance of reaching or surpassing the price of 5.3 before it expires.

You will notice that there are two volatility categories for the High Price Call Tables, and these two categories require the following yearly volatility levels for the underlying stock or ETF price.

Average volatility = 23% to 39%
High volatility   = 40% to 60%

Interpolation is required to determine the high price of options with underlying stocks that have different projected volatility than those listed above.

To the option writer, the High Price Call Tables can provide the parameters for writing strategies. For example, they can provide the bailout point for a strategy, plus indicate the percentage chance that you will be bounced out of the strategy.

You will notice by reviewing the High Price Call Tables that the further the options are out-of-the-money, the smaller the probability that high price will be reached, showing you the value of selling (writing) far out-of-the-money options.

HIGH PRICE CALL TABLE
Exercise Price is ⑩

Average Volatility

STOCK PRICE	NUMBER OF MONTHS BEFORE THE OPTIONS EXPIRE								
	1	2	3	4	5	6	7	8	9
0	0.0	0.0	0.0	0.0	0.0	0.0	0.0	0.0	0.0
0	1 %	1 %	1 %	1 %	1 %	1 %	1 %	1 %	1 %
1	0.0	0.0	0.0	0.0	0.0	0.0	0.0	0.0	0.0
1	1 %	1 %	1 %	1 %	1 %	1 %	1 %	1 %	1 %
2	0.0	0.0	0.0	0.0	0.0	0.0	0.0	0.0	0.0
2	1 %	1 %	1 %	1 %	1 %	1 %	1 %	1 %	1 %
3	0.0	0.0	0.0	0.0	0.0	0.0	0.0	0.0	0.0
3	1 %	1 %	1 %	1 %	1 %	1 %	1 %	1 %	1 %
4	0.0	0.0	0.0	0.0	0.0	0.0	0.0	0.0	0.0
4	1 %	1 %	1 %	1 %	1 %	1 %	1 %	1 %	1 %
5	0.0	0.0	0.0	0.0	0.0	0.0	0.0	0.0	0.0
5	1 %	1 %	1 %	1 %	1 %	1 %	0 %	2 %	3 %
6	0.0	0.0	0.0	0.0	0.0	0.0	0.0	0.0	0.0
6	1 %	1 %	1 %	0 %	4 %	4 %	6 %	7 %	13%
7	0.0	0.0	0.0	0.0	0.0	0.0	0.0	0.0	0.1
7	1 %	1 %	4 %	8 %	12%	18%	21%	25%	27%
8	0.0	0.0	0.0	0.0	0.1	0.1	0.2	0.2	0.3
8	1 %	8 %	21%	27%	34%	39%	38%	39%	39%
9	0.0	0.1	0.2	0.3	0.4	0.5	0.6	0.6	0.7
9	26%	39%	41%	41%	39%	41%	39%	40%	40%
10	0.4	0.6	0.7	0.9	1.0	1.1	1.1	1.2	1.3
10	35%	36%	38%	38%	41%	41%	41%	40%	39%
11	1.3	1.5	1.6	1.7	1.8	1.9	2.0	2.0	2.2
11	40%	40%	41%	41%	41%	42%	42%	43%	40%
12	2.3	2.4	2.5	2.7	2.8	2.9	2.9	3.0	3.1
12	40%	40%	40%	40%	40%	40%	40%	41%	41%
13	3.3	3.5	3.6	3.7	3.9	3.9	4.0	4.1	4.2
13	40%	41%	41%	40%	38%	40%	39%	43%	40%
14	4.3	4.5	4.6	4.8	4.9	5.0	5.1	5.2	5.3
14	40%	40%	41%	41%	39%	41%	41%	42%	41%
15	5.3	5.5	5.6	5.8	6.0	6.1	6.2	6.3	6.4
15	40%	42%	41%	42%	39%	41%	41%	41%	39%

High Volatility

STOCK PRICE	NUMBER OF MONTHS BEFORE THE OPTIONS EXPIRE								
	1	2	3	4	5	6	7	8	9
0	0.0	0.0	0.0	0.0	0.0	0.0	0.0	0.0	0.0
0	1 %	1 %	1 %	1 %	1 %	1 %	1 %	1 %	1 %
1	0.0	0.0	0.0	0.0	0.0	0.0	0.0	0.0	0.0
1	1 %	1 %	1 %	1 %	1 %	1 %	1 %	1 %	0 %
2	0.0	0.0	0.0	0.0	0.0	0.0	0.0	0.0	0.0
2	1 %	1 %	1 %	1 %	1 %	1 %	1 %	1 %	1 %
3	0.0	0.0	0.0	0.0	0.0	0.0	0.0	0.0	0.0
3	1 %	1 %	1 %	1 %	0 %	1 %	1 %	2 %	2 %
4	0.0	0.0	0.0	0.0	0.0	0.0	0.0	0.0	0.0
4	1 %	1 %	1 %	1 %	1 %	2 %	3 %	7 %	9 %
5	0.0	0.0	0.0	0.0	0.0	0.0	0.0	0.0	0.1
5	1 %	1 %	1 %	2 %	5 %	9 %	9 %	13%	16%
6	0.0	0.0	0.0	0.0	0.0	0.0	0.0	0.1	0.2
6	1 %	1 %	4 %	9 %	13%	17%	19%	24%	25%
7	0.0	0.0	0.0	0.1	0.2	0.2	0.3	0.3	0.5
7	1 %	8 %	14%	23%	25%	28%	32%	37%	34%
8	0.0	0.1	0.2	0.3	0.4	0.5	0.6	0.7	0.9
8	9 %	24%	33%	36%	35%	35%	38%	38%	35%
9	0.1	0.4	0.5	0.7	0.9	1.0	1.1	1.2	1.4
9	38%	38%	38%	36%	33%	36%	35%	40%	36%
10	0.6	1.0	1.1	1.4	1.6	1.7	1.8	1.9	2.1
10	39%	41%	39%	41%	40%	40%	40%	42%	41%
11	1.5	1.8	2.0	2.2	2.4	2.6	2.7	2.8	3.0
11	43%	43%	43%	43%	42%	42%	42%	43%	42%
12	2.5	2.8	3.0	3.2	3.4	3.6	3.6	3.8	4.0
12	43%	44%	43%	43%	43%	43%	43%	43%	43%
13	3.5	3.9	4.0	4.3	4.5	4.6	4.7	4.8	5.1
13	43%	44%	43%	43%	43%	43%	43%	44%	43%
14	4.5	4.9	5.1	5.3	5.5	5.7	5.8	5.9	6.2
14	43%	43%	43%	43%	43%	43%	44%	44%	43%
15	5.5	5.9	6.1	6.4	6.6	6.8	6.9	7.0	7.3
15	43%	43%	43%	43%	43%	41%	43%	44%	42%

HIGH PRICE CALL TABLE
Exercise Price is (15)

Average Volatility

STOCK PRICE	NUMBER OF MONTHS BEFORE THE OPTIONS EXPIRE								
	1	2	3	4	5	6	7	8	9
5	0.0	0.0	0.0	0.0	0.0	0.0	0.0	0.0	0.0
5	1 %	1 %	1 %	1 %	1 %	1 %	1 %	1 %	1 %
6	0.0	0.0	0.0	0.0	0.0	0.0	0.0	0.0	0.0
6	1 %	1 %	1 %	1 %	1 %	1 %	1 %	1 %	1 %
7	0.0	0.0	0.0	0.0	0.0	0.0	0.0	0.0	0.0
7	1 %	1 %	1 %	1 %	1 %	1 %	0 %	1 %	4 %
8	0.0	0.0	0.0	0.0	0.0	0.0	0.0	0.0	0.0
8	1 %	1 %	1 %	1 %	1 %	1 %	4 %	4 %	7 %
9	0.0	0.0	0.0	0.0	0.0	0.0	0.0	0.0	0.0
9	1 %	1 %	1 %	1 %	4 %	4 %	8 %	10%	17%
10	0.0	0.0	0.0	0.0	0.0	0.0	0.0	0.0	0.1
10	1 %	1 %	1 %	4 %	9 %	14%	20%	21%	24%
11	0.0	0.0	0.0	0.0	0.0	0.1	0.1	0.2	0.2
11	1 %	4 %	8 %	17%	22%	26%	28%	34%	37%
12	0.0	0.0	0.0	0.1	0.2	0.3	0.3	0.4	0.5
12	1 %	12%	23%	30%	37%	38%	38%	39%	39%
13	0.0	0.1	0.2	0.4	0.5	0.6	0.7	0.8	1.0
13	15%	35%	39%	39%	39%	40%	40%	39%	39%
14	0.1	0.4	0.6	0.8	1.0	1.1	1.2	1.3	1.5
14	40%	40%	39%	39%	39%	40%	38%	37%	36%
15	0.6	0.9	1.2	1.4	1.6	1.7	1.8	2.0	2.1
15	36%	38%	38%	39%	41%	40%	41%	39%	40%
16	1.5	1.8	2.0	2.3	2.4	2.6	2.7	2.8	3.0
16	41%	40%	41%	40%	39%	39%	38%	39%	41%
17	2.5	2.8	3.0	3.2	3.3	3.5	3.6	3.7	3.9
17	41%	40%	40%	41%	41%	42%	39%	38%	38%
18	3.5	3.7	3.9	4.1	4.3	4.4	4.5	4.7	4.9
18	41%	41%	40%	40%	40%	40%	40%	41%	42%
19	4.5	4.8	5.0	5.2	5.4	5.5	5.6	5.8	6.0
19	41%	40%	41%	40%	40%	41%	41%	41%	41%
20	5.5	5.8	6.0	6.2	6.4	6.5	6.7	6.9	7.0
20	40%	40%	40%	40%	41%	41%	40%	40%	41%

High Volatility

STOCK PRICE	NUMBER OF MONTHS BEFORE THE OPTIONS EXPIRE								
	1	2	3	4	5	6	7	8	9
5	0.0	0.0	0.0	0.0	0.0	0.0	0.0	0.0	0.0
5	1 %	1 %	1 %	1 %	1 %	2 %	2 %	5 %	8 %
6	0.0	0.0	0.0	0.0	0.0	0.0	0.0	0.0	0.1
6	1 %	1 %	1 %	1 %	2 %	3 %	7 %	8 %	11%
7	0.0	0.0	0.0	0.0	0.0	0.0	0.0	0.1	0.1
7	1 %	1 %	1 %	2 %	6 %	9 %	9 %	12%	14%
8	0.0	0.0	0.0	0.0	0.0	0.0	0.1	0.2	0.3
8	1 %	1 %	2 %	7 %	10%	12%	14%	19%	21%
9	0.0	0.0	0.0	0.0	0.1	0.1	0.2	0.3	0.4
9	1 %	2 %	7 %	12%	17%	19%	24%	26%	29%
10	0.0	0.0	0.0	0.1	0.2	0.3	0.4	0.5	0.7
10	1 %	7 %	12%	19%	24%	27%	29%	30%	34%
11	0.0	0.0	0.1	0.3	0.4	0.5	0.7	0.8	1.0
11	2 %	13%	23%	29%	35%	36%	37%	38%	36%
12	0.0	0.1	0.3	0.6	0.8	0.9	1.1	1.3	1.5
12	10%	26%	35%	35%	36%	36%	36%	36%	36%
13	0.1	0.4	0.7	1.0	1.3	1.4	1.6	1.8	2.1
13	26%	36%	35%	35%	33%	33%	35%	36%	37%
14	0.4	0.9	1.2	1.6	1.8	2.0	2.2	2.4	2.7
14	38%	34%	37%	39%	40%	40%	38%	37%	38%
15	1.0	1.6	1.9	2.3	2.5	2.7	2.9	3.2	3.5
15	42%	42%	39%	43%	42%	41%	41%	41%	40%
16	1.9	2.4	2.8	3.2	3.4	3.6	3.8	4.1	4.4
16	43%	43%	43%	42%	42%	41%	42%	42%	42%
17	2.9	3.4	3.7	4.1	4.4	4.5	4.7	5.0	5.3
17	43%	43%	43%	43%	43%	43%	43%	44%	43%
18	3.9	4.4	4.7	5.1	5.4	5.5	5.7	6.0	6.3
18	43%	43%	43%	44%	43%	43%	43%	44%	43%
19	4.9	5.4	5.8	6.1	6.4	6.6	6.8	7.1	7.4
19	43%	43%	43%	43%	43%	43%	43%	43%	43%
20	5.9	6.4	6.8	7.2	7.5	7.7	7.9	8.2	8.5
20	43%	43%	43%	43%	43%	43%	43%	43%	43%

HIGH PRICE CALL TABLE
Exercise Price is ⑳

Average Volatility

STOCK PRICE — NUMBER OF MONTHS BEFORE THE OPTIONS EXPIRE

STOCK PRICE	1	2	3	4	5	6	7	8	9
10	0.0	0.0	0.0	0.0	0.0	0.0	0.0	0.0	0.0
10	1 %	1 %	1 %	1 %	1 %	1 %	4 %	4 %	5 %
11	0.0	0.0	0.0	0.0	0.0	0.0	0.0	0.0	0.0
11	1 %	1 %	1 %	1 %	1 %	4 %	4 %	6 %	9 %
12	0.0	0.0	0.0	0.0	0.0	0.0	0.0	0.0	0.0
12	1 %	1 %	1 %	1 %	4 %	7 %	8 %	11%	17%
13	0.0	0.0	0.0	0.0	0.0	0.0	0.0	0.1	0.1
13	1 %	1 %	1 %	4 %	8 %	12%	17%	20%	24%
14	0.0	0.0	0.0	0.0	0.0	0.0	0.1	0.1	0.2
14	1 %	1 %	4 %	8 %	18%	22%	24%	27%	32%
15	0.0	0.0	0.0	0.0	0.1	0.2	0.3	0.4	0.5
15	1 %	4 %	12%	21%	25%	28%	34%	35%	37%
16	0.0	0.0	0.0	0.2	0.3	0.4	0.5	0.6	0.8
16	1 %	13%	25%	32%	37%	39%	39%	40%	40%
17	0.0	0.1	0.2	0.4	0.6	0.7	0.9	1.0	1.2
17	8 %	26%	37%	39%	39%	39%	41%	39%	39%
18	0.1	0.3	0.5	0.8	1.0	1.2	1.3	1.5	1.7
18	30%	39%	39%	39%	39%	39%	39%	40%	39%
19	0.3	0.7	1.0	1.3	1.5	1.7	1.9	2.1	2.3
19	40%	39%	40%	37%	36%	37%	35%	35%	36%
20	0.9	1.3	1.6	1.9	2.2	2.4	2.5	2.7	3.0
20	36%	37%	38%	40%	41%	41%	39%	40%	41%
21	1.7	2.2	2.5	2.8	3.0	3.2	3.4	3.6	3.8
21	40%	42%	42%	41%	41%	40%	41%	40%	40%
22	2.7	3.1	3.4	3.6	3.9	4.0	4.2	4.4	4.6
22	40%	40%	41%	40%	42%	41%	41%	41%	41%
23	3.7	4.1	4.3	4.6	4.9	5.0	5.2	5.4	5.6
23	41%	40%	40%	40%	40%	41%	40%	40%	40%
24	4.7	5.1	5.3	5.6	5.8	6.0	6.1	6.4	6.6
24	41%	41%	40%	41%	41%	40%	40%	40%	42%
25	5.7	6.1	6.3	6.7	6.9	7.1	7.2	7.5	7.7
25	41%	40%	40%	40%	41%	40%	41%	41%	41%

High Volatility

STOCK PRICE — NUMBER OF MONTHS BEFORE THE OPTIONS EXPIRE

STOCK PRICE	1	2	3	4	5	6	7	8	9
10	0.0	0.0	0.0	0.0	0.0	0.1	0.1	0.2	0.3
10	1 %	1 %	2 %	6 %	9 %	12%	13%	17%	19%
11	0.0	0.0	0.0	0.0	0.1	0.2	0.2	0.3	0.5
11	1 %	1 %	3 %	10%	11%	14%	18%	20%	23%
12	0.0	0.0	0.0	0.1	0.2	0.3	0.4	0.5	0.7
12	1 %	2 %	8 %	12%	17%	19%	23%	25%	30%
13	0.0	0.0	0.0	0.2	0.3	0.4	0.6	0.7	1.0
13	1 %	6 %	11%	19%	22%	25%	28%	29%	31%
14	0.0	0.0	0.1	0.3	0.5	0.6	0.8	1.0	1.2
14	1 %	11%	19%	26%	29%	34%	35%	36%	35%
15	0.0	0.1	0.3	0.6	0.8	1.0	1.1	1.4	1.7
15	3 %	19%	25%	31%	35%	35%	37%	37%	35%
16	0.0	0.2	0.5	0.8	1.1	1.3	1.5	1.8	2.1
16	12%	28%	35%	36%	37%	36%	38%	36%	33%
17	0.1	0.5	0.9	1.3	1.6	1.9	2.1	2.4	2.7
17	23%	35%	35%	36%	32%	34%	33%	37%	35%
18	0.3	0.9	1.4	1.8	2.1	2.4	2.6	2.9	3.3
18	36%	36%	34%	37%	35%	37%	37%	40%	37%
19	0.8	1.5	2.0	2.5	2.8	3.1	3.3	3.6	4.0
19	37%	37%	39%	40%	35%	35%	38%	40%	41%
20	1.4	2.2	2.7	3.2	3.5	3.8	4.1	4.4	4.8
20	42%	40%	40%	42%	42%	42%	42%	40%	37%
21	2.3	3.0	3.5	4.0	4.4	4.7	4.9	5.2	5.7
21	43%	43%	44%	43%	41%	40%	41%	42%	40%
22	3.3	4.0	4.4	5.0	5.3	5.6	5.8	6.1	6.6
22	43%	43%	43%	43%	44%	43%	43%	43%	43%
23	4.3	5.0	5.4	6.0	6.3	6.6	6.8	7.1	7.6
23	43%	43%	43%	43%	43%	43%	43%	43%	43%
24	5.2	6.0	6.4	6.9	7.3	7.6	7.8	8.1	8.6
24	43%	43%	43%	44%	43%	43%	43%	43%	43%
25	6.3	7.0	7.5	8.0	8.3	8.6	8.9	9.2	9.7
25	43%	43%	43%	43%	43%	43%	43%	43%	43%

HIGH PRICE CALL TABLE
Exercise Price is (25)

Average Volatility

STOCK PRICE — NUMBER OF MONTHS BEFORE THE OPTIONS EXPIRE

STOCK PRICE	1	2	3	4	5	6	7	8	9
15	0.0	0.0	0.0	0.0	0.0	0.0	0.0	0.0	0.1
15	1%	1%	1%	3%	4%	7%	9%	12%	19%
16	0.0	0.0	0.0	0.0	0.0	0.0	0.0	0.1	0.2
16	1%	1%	1%	4%	8%	10%	16%	20%	23%
17	0.0	0.0	0.0	0.0	0.0	0.1	0.1	0.2	0.3
17	1%	1%	4%	8%	14%	20%	22%	24%	26%
18	0.0	0.0	0.0	0.0	0.1	0.1	0.2	0.3	0.5
18	1%	4%	6%	17%	21%	24%	26%	31%	35%
19	0.0	0.0	0.0	0.1	0.2	0.3	0.4	0.5	0.7
19	1%	5%	18%	24%	29%	33%	37%	38%	39%
20	0.0	0.0	0.1	0.3	0.4	0.5	0.7	0.9	1.1
20	1%	16%	24%	32%	35%	37%	39%	39%	39%
21	0.0	0.1	0.2	0.5	0.7	0.9	1.0	1.2	1.5
21	7%	24%	35%	39%	39%	39%	39%	39%	40%
22	0.0	0.3	0.5	0.8	1.1	1.3	1.5	1.7	1.9
22	22%	38%	40%	40%	40%	39%	39%	39%	39%
23	0.2	0.6	0.9	1.3	1.6	1.8	2.0	2.2	2.5
23	39%	39%	39%	38%	38%	39%	38%	37%	35%
24	0.6	1.1	1.5	1.8	2.1	2.4	2.6	2.8	3.1
24	39%	38%	36%	35%	37%	35%	35%	37%	38%
25	1.1	1.7	2.1	2.5	2.8	3.0	3.2	3.5	3.8
25	36%	38%	38%	40%	43%	40%	39%	40%	41%
26	2.0	2.5	2.9	3.3	3.6	3.8	4.1	4.4	4.7
26	40%	42%	43%	41%	39%	42%	42%	42%	41%
27	2.9	3.5	3.8	4.2	4.5	4.7	5.0	5.2	5.5
27	40%	41%	40%	40%	41%	40%	41%	41%	39%
28	3.9	4.4	4.8	5.1	5.4	5.6	5.8	6.1	6.4
28	41%	40%	40%	40%	41%	42%	41%	40%	38%
29	4.9	5.4	5.8	6.1	6.4	6.6	6.8	7.1	7.4
29	42%	41%	40%	40%	40%	40%	40%	40%	40%
30	5.9	6.4	6.7	7.1	7.4	7.6	7.8	8.0	8.4
30	41%	41%	40%	40%	40%	40%	40%	40%	40%

High Volatility

STOCK PRICE — NUMBER OF MONTHS BEFORE THE OPTIONS EXPIRE

STOCK PRICE	1	2	3	4	5	6	7	8	9
15	0.0	0.0	0.0	0.1	0.3	0.4	0.5	0.7	0.9
15	1%	2%	9%	13%	17%	19%	24%	26%	29%
16	0.0	0.0	0.1	0.3	0.4	0.6	0.7	0.9	1.2
16	1%	6%	12%	17%	20%	24%	28%	29%	32%
17	0.0	0.0	0.1	0.4	0.6	0.7	0.9	1.2	1.5
17	0%	9%	16%	20%	26%	30%	32%	36%	35%
18	0.0	0.1	0.3	0.6	0.8	1.0	1.3	1.6	1.9
18	2%	13%	19%	27%	31%	32%	35%	36%	34%
19	0.0	0.2	0.4	0.8	1.1	1.3	1.6	2.0	2.3
19	6%	20%	29%	33%	35%	35%	35%	35%	32%
20	0.0	0.4	0.7	1.2	1.5	1.8	2.1	2.4	2.8
20	12%	26%	34%	36%	36%	36%	36%	35%	33%
21	0.1	0.6	1.0	1.6	2.0	2.3	2.6	2.9	3.4
21	19%	35%	37%	37%	34%	33%	33%	35%	35%
22	0.3	1.0	1.5	2.1	2.5	2.8	3.2	3.6	4.0
22	36%	35%	36%	34%	37%	36%	36%	36%	36%
23	0.7	1.5	2.1	2.7	3.1	3.4	3.8	4.2	4.6
23	36%	35%	37%	37%	38%	40%	37%	36%	38%
24	1.2	2.1	2.7	3.3	3.8	4.1	4.4	4.9	5.4
24	35%	37%	41%	36%	36%	39%	39%	40%	40%
25	1.8	2.8	3.4	4.1	4.6	4.9	5.2	5.7	6.2
25	42%	41%	42%	42%	42%	42%	42%	40%	36%
26	2.7	3.6	4.2	4.9	5.4	5.7	6.1	6.5	7.0
26	43%	43%	43%	43%	41%	40%	39%	39%	40%
27	3.6	4.6	5.2	5.9	6.3	6.6	7.0	7.4	8.0
27	43%	43%	43%	43%	42%	43%	43%	42%	42%
28	4.6	5.5	6.1	6.8	7.3	7.6	7.9	8.4	8.9
28	44%	43%	43%	43%	43%	43%	43%	43%	43%
29	5.6	6.5	7.1	7.8	8.3	8.6	8.9	9.4	9.9
29	44%	43%	43%	43%	43%	43%	43%	43%	43%
30	6.6	7.5	8.1	8.8	9.3	9.6	9.9	10.	10.
30	43%	43%	43%	43%	43%	43%	43%	43%	43%

HIGH PRICE CALL TABLE
Exercise Price is (30)

Average Volatility

STOCK PRICE — NUMBER OF MONTHS BEFORE THE OPTIONS EXPIRE

STOCK PRICE	1	2	3	4	5	6	7	8	9
20	0.0	0.0	0.0	0.0	0.0	0.1	0.1	0.2	0.3
20	1 %	1 %	4 %	7 %	10%	18%	19%	25%	25%
21	0.0	0.0	0.0	0.0	0.1	0.2	0.2	0.4	0.5
21	1 %	1 %	4 %	10%	20%	23%	25%	26%	31%
22	0.0	0.0	0.0	0.1	0.2	0.3	0.4	0.5	0.7
22	1 %	4 %	9 %	20%	25%	26%	30%	34%	35%
23	0.0	0.0	0.0	0.2	0.3	0.4	0.6	0.8	1.0
23	1 %	7 %	19%	24%	30%	34%	35%	37%	38%
24	0.0	0.0	0.1	0.3	0.5	0.6	0.8	1.0	1.3
24	1 %	17%	24%	32%	37%	39%	39%	39%	40%
25	0.0	0.1	0.3	0.6	0.8	1.0	1.2	1.5	1.7
25	5 %	24%	33%	36%	40%	39%	39%	40%	39%
26	0.0	0.2	0.5	0.9	1.1	1.4	1.6	1.9	2.1
26	18%	34%	39%	39%	39%	40%	39%	39%	39%
27	0.1	0.5	0.9	1.3	1.6	1.9	2.1	2.4	2.7
27	33%	40%	39%	39%	38%	38%	39%	38%	38%
28	0.4	0.9	1.3	1.8	2.1	2.4	2.6	3.0	3.3
28	39%	39%	39%	36%	37%	36%	36%	34%	35%
29	0.8	1.4	1.9	2.4	2.7	3.0	3.2	3.5	3.9
29	40%	40%	37%	36%	36%	35%	39%	39%	38%
30	1.4	2.1	2.5	3.0	3.4	3.7	3.9	4.2	4.6
30	37%	38%	38%	40%	43%	41%	40%	42%	41%
31	2.2	2.9	3.3	3.8	4.2	4.5	4.7	5.1	5.5
31	41%	42%	43%	41%	41%	42%	41%	42%	42%
32	3.2	3.8	4.2	4.8	5.1	5.4	5.6	6.0	6.4
32	40%	41%	40%	40%	40%	40%	39%	39%	39%
33	4.1	4.7	5.1	5.6	5.9	6.2	6.4	6.8	7.2
33	41%	40%	40%	40%	41%	41%	41%	42%	41%
34	5.1	5.7	6.1	6.6	6.9	7.2	7.4	7.8	8.2
34	41%	40%	40%	40%	41%	40%	41%	41%	38%
35	6.1	6.7	7.1	7.6	7.9	8.2	8.4	8.8	9.1
35	41%	41%	40%	40%	40%	40%	40%	40%	40%

High Volatility

STOCK PRICE — NUMBER OF MONTHS BEFORE THE OPTIONS EXPIRE

STOCK PRICE	1	2	3	4	5	6	7	8	9
20	0.0	0.0	0.2	0.4	0.7	0.9	1.1	1.4	1.7
20	1 %	8 %	14%	20%	26%	29%	30%	32%	33%
21	0.0	0.1	0.3	0.6	0.9	1.1	1.4	1.7	2.1
21	1 %	12%	20%	26%	30%	31%	34%	35%	35%
22	0.0	0.1	0.4	0.8	1.1	1.4	1.7	2.1	2.5
22	2 %	16%	25%	31%	33%	35%	35%	35%	34%
23	0.0	0.3	0.6	1.1	1.5	1.8	2.1	2.5	3.0
23	7 %	20%	30%	31%	33%	35%	35%	36%	32%
24	0.0	0.4	0.9	1.4	1.9	2.2	2.6	3.0	3.5
24	12%	29%	34%	36%	34%	36%	35%	32%	32%
25	0.1	0.7	1.2	1.9	2.3	2.7	3.0	3.5	4.0
25	20%	33%	35%	34%	32%	32%	33%	35%	36%
26	0.3	1.0	1.7	2.4	2.9	3.2	3.6	4.1	4.6
26	30%	36%	36%	34%	35%	36%	36%	37%	38%
27	0.6	1.5	2.2	2.9	3.5	3.8	4.2	4.7	5.3
27	36%	36%	33%	35%	35%	37%	39%	36%	37%
28	1.0	2.0	2.8	3.5	4.1	4.5	4.8	5.4	5.9
28	37%	34%	37%	40%	37%	35%	38%	39%	40%
29	1.6	2.7	3.4	4.2	4.8	5.2	5.6	6.1	6.7
29	34%	38%	40%	37%	38%	41%	40%	40%	41%
30	2.2	3.5	4.2	5.0	5.5	5.9	6.3	6.9	7.5
30	42%	40%	41%	42%	42%	42%	42%	38%	37%
31	3.1	4.2	5.0	5.8	6.4	6.8	7.2	7.8	8.4
31	43%	43%	43%	43%	41%	39%	41%	39%	39%
32	4.1	5.2	5.9	6.7	7.3	7.7	8.1	8.7	9.3
32	43%	43%	43%	43%	42%	42%	42%	42%	42%
33	5.0	6.1	6.9	7.6	8.2	8.6	9.0	9.6	10.
33	43%	43%	43%	43%	43%	43%	44%	43%	43%
34	6.0	7.1	7.8	8.6	9.2	9.6	10.	10.	11.
34	43%	43%	44%	43%	43%	43%	44%	43%	43%
35	7.0	8.1	8.8	9.6	10.	10.	11.	11.	12.
35	43%	43%	43%	43%	43%	43%	43%	43%	43%

HIGH PRICE CALL TABLE
Exercise Price is (35)

Average Volatility

STOCK PRICE

NUMBER OF MONTHS BEFORE THE OPTIONS EXPIRE

STOCK PRICE	1	2	3	4	5	6	7	8	9
25	0.0	0.0	0.0	0.1	0.1	0.2	0.4	0.5	0.7
25	1 %	4 %	7 %	16%	21%	25%	26%	31%	32%
26	0.0	0.0	0.0	0.1	0.3	0.4	0.5	0.7	0.9
26	1 %	4 %	11%	21%	25%	27%	32%	34%	35%
27	0.0	0.0	0.1	0.2	0.4	0.6	0.7	1.0	1.2
27	1 %	9 %	19%	24%	32%	34%	36%	38%	39%
28	0.0	0.0	0.2	0.4	0.6	0.8	1.0	1.3	1.6
28	2 %	17%	24%	32%	35%	38%	39%	39%	39%
29	0.0	0.1	0.3	0.6	0.9	1.1	1.3	1.6	2.0
29	4 %	25%	33%	38%	39%	39%	39%	39%	39%
30	0.0	0.2	0.6	0.9	1.2	1.5	1.8	2.1	2.4
30	12%	32%	38%	39%	40%	39%	39%	39%	38%
31	0.1	0.5	0.9	1.3	1.6	2.0	2.2	2.5	2.9
31	25%	38%	39%	40%	39%	39%	39%	39%	38%
32	0.2	0.8	1.3	1.8	2.2	2.4	2.7	3.1	3.5
32	38%	40%	39%	38%	37%	38%	39%	37%	35%
33	0.6	1.3	1.8	2.3	2.7	3.0	3.3	3.7	4.1
33	39%	38%	38%	36%	36%	35%	35%	35%	35%
34	1.0	1.8	2.3	2.9	3.3	3.6	3.9	4.3	4.7
34	39%	36%	36%	35%	37%	38%	40%	40%	39%
35	1.6	2.4	3.0	3.6	4.0	4.3	4.6	5.0	5.5
35	37%	39%	38%	40%	43%	41%	40%	43%	43%
36	2.4	3.2	3.8	4.4	4.8	5.1	5.4	5.9	6.3
36	40%	41%	41%	41%	42%	42%	43%	42%	42%
37	3.4	4.2	4.7	5.3	5.7	6.0	6.4	6.8	7.2
37	40%	41%	40%	41%	40%	38%	39%	40%	38%
38	4.4	5.1	5.6	6.2	6.6	6.9	7.2	7.6	8.0
38	40%	41%	40%	41%	40%	40%	41%	38%	38%
39	5.3	6.1	6.6	7.1	7.5	7.8	8.1	8.5	8.9
39	41%	40%	40%	40%	42%	41%	42%	43%	39%
40	6.3	7.1	7.5	8.1	8.5	8.8	9.1	9.5	9.9
40	41%	40%	41%	41%	40%	40%	40%	41%	40%

High Volatility

STOCK PRICE

NUMBER OF MONTHS BEFORE THE OPTIONS EXPIRE

STOCK PRICE	1	2	3	4	5	6	7	8	9
25	0.0	0.1	0.4	0.9	1.2	1.5	1.8	2.2	2.7
25	4 %	20%	24%	31%	32%	32%	32%	32%	32%
26	0.0	0.2	0.6	1.1	1.5	1.8	2.1	2.6	3.1
26	3 %	23%	26%	32%	32%	33%	34%	33%	32%
27	0.0	0.4	0.8	1.4	1.8	2.2	2.6	3.1	3.6
27	9 %	25%	32%	32%	32%	34%	33%	32%	33%
28	0.0	0.6	1.1	1.8	2.3	2.6	3.0	3.6	4.1
28	15%	31%	32%	32%	32%	32%	34%	35%	34%
29	0.1	0.8	1.4	2.2	2.7	3.1	3.6	4.1	4.7
29	23%	33%	32%	32%	33%	34%	34%	35%	35%
30	0.3	1.1	1.8	2.7	3.2	3.6	4.1	4.6	5.3
30	30%	32%	32%	34%	35%	35%	36%	35%	35%
31	0.5	1.5	2.3	3.2	3.8	4.2	4.7	5.3	5.9
31	33%	32%	35%	36%	35%	37%	35%	35%	36%
32	0.9	2.1	2.9	3.8	4.4	4.8	5.3	5.9	6.6
32	33%	36%	34%	37%	35%	36%	36%	37%	38%
33	1.4	2.6	3.5	4.4	5.1	5.5	6.0	6.6	7.2
33	35%	37%	37%	37%	38%	37%	38%	38%	39%
34	2.0	3.3	4.2	5.1	5.8	6.2	6.7	7.4	8.0
34	36%	39%	39%	40%	39%	40%	39%	40%	37%
35	2.6	4.0	4.9	5.9	6.5	7.0	7.5	8.1	8.8
35	40%	40%	40%	41%	40%	40%	39%	39%	39%
36	3.5	4.8	5.7	6.7	7.4	7.8	8.3	9.0	9.7
36	41%	40%	40%	40%	41%	40%	40%	40%	40%
37	4.4	5.8	6.6	7.7	8.3	8.7	9.2	9.9	10.
37	42%	41%	40%	41%	40%	40%	40%	41%	40%
38	5.4	6.7	7.6	8.6	9.2	9.7	10.	10.	11.
38	41%	41%	40%	40%	40%	40%	40%	40%	40%
39	6.4	7.7	8.5	9.5	10.	10.	11.	11.	12.
39	42%	41%	41%	40%	40%	40%	40%	40%	41%
40	7.4	8.7	9.5	10.	11.	11.	12.	12.	13.
40	41%	41%	41%	40%	40%	40%	40%	40%	40%

HIGH PRICE CALL TABLE
Exercise Price is ⑩

Average Volatility

STOCK PRICE — NUMBER OF MONTHS BEFORE THE OPTIONS EXPIRE

	1	2	3	4	5	6	7	8	9
30	0.0	0.0	0.0	0.2	0.3	0.5	0.7	0.9	1.2
30	1%	4%	13%	22%	26%	30%	33%	35%	36%
31	0.0	0.0	0.1	0.3	0.5	0.7	0.9	1.2	1.5
31	1%	9%	19%	25%	31%	34%	35%	38%	38%
32	0.0	0.0	0.2	0.4	0.7	0.9	1.2	1.5	1.8
32	1%	18%	24%	32%	35%	38%	40%	40%	39%
33	0.0	0.1	0.3	0.7	1.0	1.3	1.5	1.9	2.2
33	4%	22%	32%	36%	38%	40%	39%	39%	39%
34	0.0	0.2	0.5	1.0	1.3	1.6	1.9	2.3	2.7
34	10%	31%	38%	39%	39%	39%	40%	40%	38%
35	0.0	0.4	0.9	1.3	1.8	2.1	2.4	2.7	3.1
35	21%	37%	39%	39%	38%	39%	39%	39%	38%
36	0.2	0.7	1.2	1.8	2.2	2.5	2.8	3.2	3.7
36	33%	39%	39%	39%	38%	38%	39%	38%	36%
37	0.4	1.1	1.7	2.3	2.7	3.1	3.4	3.8	4.3
37	39%	39%	39%	37%	37%	37%	36%	36%	35%
38	0.8	1.6	2.2	2.8	3.3	3.7	4.0	4.4	4.9
38	39%	39%	37%	36%	35%	35%	35%	36%	36%
39	1.3	2.2	2.8	3.4	3.9	4.3	4.6	5.0	5.5
39	40%	36%	36%	37%	39%	38%	40%	39%	38%
40	1.9	2.8	3.4	4.1	4.6	5.0	5.3	5.7	6.3
40	37%	38%	39%	42%	42%	41%	41%	44%	43%
41	2.7	3.6	4.2	4.9	5.4	5.8	6.1	6.6	7.2
41	40%	41%	42%	42%	42%	42%	42%	42%	42%
42	3.6	4.5	5.1	5.8	6.3	6.7	7.1	7.5	8.0
42	40%	42%	41%	41%	39%	40%	40%	39%	39%
43	4.6	5.5	6.1	6.7	7.2	7.5	7.9	8.3	8.9
43	41%	40%	40%	41%	40%	40%	40%	42%	38%
44	5.5	6.4	7.0	7.6	8.0	8.4	8.7	9.1	9.6
44	41%	40%	40%	40%	41%	41%	41%	43%	41%
45	6.5	7.4	7.9	8.6	9.0	9.4	9.7	10.	10.
45	42%	40%	40%	40%	41%	41%	40%	40%	39%

High Volatility

STOCK PRICE — NUMBER OF MONTHS BEFORE THE OPTIONS EXPIRE

	1	2	3	4	5	6	7	8	9
30	0.0	0.3	0.8	1.4	1.8	2.2	2.6	3.1	3.9
30	7%	23%	30%	32%	32%	32%	33%	32%	33%
31	0.0	0.5	1.0	1.7	2.2	2.6	3.0	3.6	4.3
31	11%	25%	32%	33%	32%	33%	32%	34%	34%
32	0.1	0.6	1.3	2.0	2.6	3.1	3.6	4.1	4.8
32	16%	33%	33%	33%	32%	32%	33%	34%	34%
33	0.2	0.9	1.7	2.5	3.1	3.6	4.1	4.6	5.4
33	23%	32%	32%	32%	34%	34%	34%	35%	35%
34	0.3	1.2	2.0	3.0	3.6	4.1	4.6	5.2	6.0
34	27%	32%	33%	35%	35%	35%	35%	36%	35%
35	0.5	1.6	2.5	3.5	4.1	4.6	5.2	5.8	6.6
35	32%	32%	34%	36%	35%	35%	35%	35%	35%
36	0.8	2.1	3.1	4.0	4.7	5.3	5.8	6.4	7.3
36	34%	35%	36%	35%	36%	35%	34%	36%	37%
37	1.2	2.7	3.6	4.7	5.4	5.9	6.5	7.1	8.0
37	34%	35%	36%	37%	37%	37%	37%	39%	38%
38	1.8	3.2	4.3	5.3	6.0	6.6	7.1	7.8	8.6
38	35%	37%	38%	37%	37%	37%	38%	38%	38%
39	2.4	3.9	4.9	6.0	6.7	7.3	7.9	8.6	9.5
39	38%	40%	38%	40%	40%	40%	39%	39%	38%
40	3.1	4.6	5.7	6.8	7.5	8.1	8.7	9.3	10.
40	40%	40%	40%	40%	40%	40%	39%	39%	39%
41	3.9	5.5	6.5	7.6	8.3	8.9	9.5	10.	11.
41	41%	40%	40%	40%	40%	40%	40%	40%	40%
42	4.8	6.4	7.4	8.5	9.3	9.8	10.	11.	12.
42	42%	41%	40%	40%	40%	40%	41%	40%	40%
43	5.8	7.3	8.4	9.5	10.	10.	11.	12.	13.
43	41%	41%	40%	40%	40%	40%	40%	40%	40%
44	6.8	8.3	9.3	10.	11.	11.	12.	12.	13.
44	41%	41%	41%	40%	40%	41%	41%	40%	40%
45	7.8	9.3	10.	11.	12.	12.	13.	13.	14.
45	42%	41%	41%	40%	40%	40%	40%	40%	40%

HIGH PRICE CALL TABLE
Exercise Price is (45)

Average Volatility

STOCK PRICE

NUMBER OF MONTHS BEFORE THE OPTIONS EXPIRE

	1	2	3	4	5	6	7	8	9
35	0.0	0.0	0.2	0.4	0.7	0.9	1.1	1.3	1.8
35	1%	10%	20%	27%	30%	34%	35%	39%	39%
36	0.0	0.1	0.3	0.6	0.9	1.1	1.4	1.7	2.1
36	2%	17%	24%	31%	32%	37%	38%	40%	38%
37	0.0	0.1	0.4	0.7	1.2	1.4	1.8	2.0	2.5
37	4%	22%	31%	36%	36%	39%	39%	39%	39%
38	0.0	0.3	0.6	1.1	1.5	1.8	2.2	2.5	3.0
38	9%	26%	34%	39%	37%	39%	38%	39%	38%
39	0.0	0.4	0.9	1.4	1.9	2.2	2.6	2.9	3.4
39	20%	34%	39%	39%	37%	39%	39%	39%	37%
40	0.2	0.7	1.2	1.8	2.4	2.7	3.1	3.4	3.9
40	25%	38%	39%	39%	36%	38%	38%	38%	36%
41	0.3	1.0	1.6	2.2	2.9	3.1	3.6	3.9	4.5
41	35%	39%	39%	39%	36%	37%	35%	39%	34%
42	0.7	1.5	2.1	2.8	3.4	3.7	4.2	4.5	5.1
42	39%	38%	38%	37%	34%	34%	35%	36%	34%
43	1.1	2.0	2.6	3.3	4.1	4.4	4.8	5.1	5.7
43	38%	36%	36%	36%	35%	36%	34%	39%	36%
44	1.6	2.6	3.2	4.0	4.7	4.9	5.4	5.7	6.4
44	36%	36%	36%	37%	36%	39%	40%	40%	38%
45	2.2	3.2	3.9	4.6	5.4	5.7	6.1	6.5	7.1
45	36%	38%	38%	41%	37%	41%	40%	43%	43%
46	3.0	4.0	4.7	5.4	6.1	6.5	7.0	7.3	8.0
46	40%	40%	43%	41%	40%	41%	42%	42%	41%
47	3.9	4.9	5.6	6.3	7.1	7.4	7.9	8.1	8.8
47	40%	42%	43%	41%	38%	41%	40%	40%	39%
48	4.9	5.9	6.5	7.2	8.0	8.3	8.7	9.0	9.8
48	40%	41%	41%	40%	38%	40%	38%	41%	38%
49	5.9	6.8	7.4	8.1	8.9	9.1	9.5	9.9	10.
49	40%	40%	40%	40%	40%	40%	40%	40%	39%
50	6.8	7.7	8.3	9.0	9.8	10.	10.	10.	11.
50	40%	41%	40%	40%	38%	41%	39%	43%	39%

High Volatility

STOCK PRICE

NUMBER OF MONTHS BEFORE THE OPTIONS EXPIRE

	1	2	3	4	5	6	7	8	9
35	0.1	0.6	1.2	1.9	2.8	3.1	3.7	4.1	5.1
35	12%	26%	32%	33%	32%	32%	32%	33%	34%
36	0.1	0.8	1.5	2.3	3.2	3.5	4.2	4.6	5.5
36	14%	31%	32%	32%	32%	33%	33%	34%	34%
37	0.2	1.0	1.8	2.7	3.7	4.0	4.7	5.1	6.2
37	23%	32%	32%	32%	33%	34%	34%	35%	35%
38	0.4	1.4	2.2	3.2	4.2	4.5	5.2	5.7	6.8
38	25%	32%	32%	35%	32%	35%	35%	35%	35%
39	0.6	1.7	2.7	3.8	4.8	5.1	5.8	6.3	7.3
39	32%	32%	34%	35%	34%	35%	34%	35%	35%
40	0.9	2.2	3.2	4.3	5.4	5.7	6.4	6.9	7.9
40	33%	32%	35%	35%	35%	36%	35%	36%	36%
41	1.2	2.7	3.8	4.9	6.0	6.4	7.1	7.5	8.7
41	32%	35%	34%	37%	35%	35%	33%	38%	38%
42	1.7	3.3	4.3	5.5	6.7	7.0	7.8	8.2	9.4
42	33%	34%	37%	37%	34%	37%	38%	39%	37%
43	2.3	3.9	5.0	6.2	7.4	7.7	8.4	8.9	10.
43	31%	37%	38%	37%	37%	38%	38%	40%	38%
44	2.9	4.6	5.7	6.9	8.1	8.4	9.2	9.7	10.
44	35%	40%	39%	40%	37%	41%	38%	37%	36%
45	3.6	5.3	6.4	7.7	8.9	9.2	10.	10.	11.
45	40%	40%	40%	40%	39%	40%	38%	39%	38%
46	4.4	6.1	7.2	8.5	9.7	10.	10.	11.	12.
46	40%	40%	41%	40%	39%	41%	39%	40%	40%
47	5.4	7.0	8.1	9.4	10.	11.	11.	12.	13.
47	40%	40%	40%	40%	40%	40%	40%	40%	40%
48	6.3	8.0	9.0	10.	11.	11.	12.	13.	14.
48	40%	42%	42%	40%	40%	40%	40%	40%	40%
49	7.3	8.9	9.9	11.	12.	12.	13.	14.	15.
49	40%	41%	41%	40%	40%	40%	40%	40%	40%
50	8.3	9.9	10.	12.	13.	13.	14.	15.	16.
50	40%	42%	41%	40%	40%	40%	40%	40%	40%

HIGH PRICE CALL TABLE
Exercise Price is ⑤⓪

Average Volatility

STOCK PRICE	NUMBER OF MONTHS BEFORE THE OPTIONS EXPIRE								
	1	2	3	4	5	6	7	8	9
35	0.0	0.0	0.0	0.1	0.2	0.3	0.5	0.7	0.9
35	1%	1%	4%	11%	17%	21%	24%	25%	28%
36	0.0	0.0	0.0	0.1	0.2	0.4	0.5	0.7	1.0
36	1%	4%	6%	18%	21%	25%	26%	31%	34%
37	0.0	0.0	0.0	0.2	0.4	0.5	0.7	1.0	1.3
37	1%	4%	9%	20%	25%	26%	31%	35%	34%
38	0.0	0.0	0.0	0.2	0.4	0.7	0.9	1.2	1.5
38	1%	5%	17%	25%	27%	32%	35%	37%	39%
39	0.0	0.0	0.1	0.4	0.6	0.9	1.1	1.5	1.8
39	1%	9%	19%	26%	32%	35%	37%	39%	39%
40	0.0	0.1	0.2	0.5	0.8	1.1	1.3	1.6	2.0
40	1%	14%	25%	32%	35%	39%	39%	39%	39%
41	0.0	0.1	0.4	0.8	1.1	1.4	1.8	2.2	2.6
41	3%	21%	29%	35%	38%	39%	39%	39%	40%
42	0.0	0.2	0.5	0.9	1.3	1.6	1.9	2.3	2.7
42	6%	24%	35%	39%	39%	41%	41%	41%	39%
43	0.0	0.4	0.9	1.4	1.8	2.2	2.6	3.0	3.5
43	13%	30%	37%	38%	39%	39%	39%	39%	38%
44	0.1	0.6	1.0	1.6	2.1	2.4	2.8	3.2	3.7
44	22%	38%	39%	40%	39%	40%	40%	39%	39%
45	0.2	0.9	1.5	2.2	2.7	3.1	3.5	4.0	4.6
45	29%	39%	39%	40%	38%	39%	39%	38%	35%
46	0.4	1.2	1.8	2.5	3.0	3.4	3.8	4.3	4.8
46	39%	39%	41%	39%	39%	40%	40%	41%	37%
47	0.8	1.8	2.5	3.2	3.8	4.3	4.7	5.2	5.8
47	39%	38%	38%	35%	35%	34%	34%	34%	33%
48	1.1	2.1	2.9	3.6	4.2	4.6	5.0	5.5	6.0
48	40%	39%	40%	38%	37%	37%	38%	39%	39%
49	1.7	2.8	3.6	4.4	5.0	5.5	5.9	6.4	6.9
49	39%	36%	36%	35%	38%	39%	40%	39%	38%
50	2.3	3.4	4.1	4.9	5.4	5.9	6.3	6.8	7.5
50	37%	38%	39%	44%	43%	42%	41%	43%	43%
51	3.0	4.2	4.9	5.7	6.4	6.9	7.3	7.9	8.5
51	40%	40%	43%	41%	42%	42%	43%	43%	41%
52	3.9	5.0	5.7	6.5	7.0	7.5	8.0	8.6	9.2
52	42%	43%	44%	43%	43%	43%	42%	42%	41%
53	4.9	6.0	6.7	7.5	8.1	8.6	9.1	9.5	10.
53	42%	41%	41%	40%	40%	41%	39%	40%	40%
54	5.9	6.9	7.6	8.3	8.9	9.3	9.8	10.	10.
54	41%	41%	40%	40%	40%	41%	41%	42%	41%
55	6.8	7.8	8.5	9.2	9.8	10.	10.	11.	11.
55	41%	41%	40%	41%	41%	42%	42%	44%	41%

High Volatility

STOCK PRICE	NUMBER OF MONTHS BEFORE THE OPTIONS EXPIRE								
	1	2	3	4	5	6	7	8	9
35	0.0	0.2	0.5	1.1	1.5	1.9	2.3	2.8	3.4
35	3%	14%	23%	25%	31%	32%	32%	32%	33%
36	0.0	0.2	0.6	1.2	1.6	2.0	2.4	2.9	3.5
36	4%	19%	24%	30%	32%	33%	33%	33%	34%
37	0.0	0.3	0.8	1.5	2.0	2.4	2.9	3.6	4.2
37	4%	22%	27%	32%	32%	33%	33%	34%	32%
38	0.0	0.4	1.0	1.7	2.3	2.7	3.2	3.8	4.5
38	8%	24%	32%	32%	32%	33%	34%	34%	35%
39	0.0	0.6	1.2	2.0	2.7	3.2	3.7	4.5	5.2
39	10%	25%	32%	32%	32%	33%	33%	33%	33%
40	0.1	0.7	1.4	2.3	2.9	3.4	3.9	4.7	5.4
40	14%	31%	33%	34%	34%	34%	34%	35%	35%
41	0.2	1.0	1.8	2.8	3.5	4.0	4.7	5.4	6.1
41	21%	32%	34%	32%	32%	33%	33%	34%	35%
42	0.3	1.2	2.0	3.1	3.8	4.4	5.0	5.7	6.5
42	26%	34%	35%	35%	35%	37%	36%	35%	35%
43	0.5	1.7	2.6	3.7	4.6	5.1	5.7	6.5	7.4
43	29%	32%	34%	34%	35%	35%	35%	35%	36%
44	0.6	1.9	2.9	4.1	4.8	5.4	6.0	6.9	7.6
44	33%	34%	35%	35%	35%	37%	36%	36%	36%
45	1.0	2.5	3.6	4.8	5.7	6.3	7.0	7.8	8.6
45	33%	34%	35%	35%	36%	35%	35%	35%	38%
46	1.3	2.9	4.0	5.2	6.1	6.7	7.3	8.2	8.9
46	36%	36%	35%	37%	38%	38%	38%	39%	40%
47	1.9	3.7	4.8	6.1	7.0	7.7	8.3	9.1	10.
47	35%	34%	37%	37%	36%	37%	38%	38%	40%
48	2.3	4.2	5.3	6.6	7.5	8.1	8.7	9.6	10.
48	35%	37%	40%	38%	38%	40%	39%	40%	40%
49	3.0	4.9	6.1	7.4	8.3	8.9	9.6	10.	11.
49	37%	40%	39%	40%	40%	40%	40%	40%	37%
50	3.6	5.5	6.7	8.1	8.9	9.6	10.	11.	12.
50	41%	41%	41%	40%	40%	40%	40%	40%	40%
51	4.4	6.4	7.6	9.0	9.9	10.	11.	12.	13.
51	41%	41%	40%	40%	40%	40%	41%	41%	40%
52	5.3	7.1	8.3	9.7	10.	11.	11.	12.	13.
52	41%	41%	41%	41%	40%	40%	40%	40%	40%
53	6.3	8.1	9.3	10.	11.	12.	13.	13.	14.
53	41%	41%	41%	40%	40%	40%	40%	40%	40%
54	7.2	9.1	10.	11.	12.	13.	13.	14.	15.
54	41%	41%	41%	41%	41%	40%	40%	40%	40%
55	8.2	10.	11.	12.	13.	14.	14.	15.	16.
55	41%	42%	42%	41%	40%	41%	40%	40%	40%

HIGH PRICE CALL TABLE

Exercise Price is (60)

Average Volatility

STOCK PRICE	NUMBER OF MONTHS BEFORE THE OPTIONS EXPIRE								
	1	2	3	4	5	6	7	8	9
45	0.0	0.0	0.1	0.4	0.6	0.8	1.1	1.4	1.8
45	1%	4%	12%	21%	24%	28%	32%	34%	36%
46	0.0	0.0	0.1	0.4	0.7	0.9	1.1	1.5	1.8
46	1%	6%	19%	25%	29%	34%	37%	39%	39%
47	0.0	0.0	0.2	0.6	0.9	1.2	1.5	1.9	2.4
47	0%	9%	21%	26%	32%	34%	37%	39%	39%
48	0.0	0.0	0.3	0.7	1.1	1.4	1.7	2.1	2.5
48	1%	17%	24%	32%	35%	38%	39%	39%	39%
49	0.0	0.1	0.4	0.9	1.3	1.7	2.1	2.6	3.1
49	4%	19%	27%	35%	38%	39%	39%	39%	39%
50	0.0	0.2	0.6	1.1	1.5	1.9	2.3	2.8	3.3
50	5%	25%	35%	38%	40%	39%	39%	40%	39%
51	0.0	0.4	0.9	1.5	2.0	2.5	2.9	3.4	4.0
51	9%	28%	35%	39%	39%	39%	39%	39%	39%
52	0.0	0.5	1.0	1.6	2.2	2.6	3.0	3.6	4.1
52	18%	35%	39%	40%	40%	39%	41%	39%	39%
53	0.2	0.9	1.5	2.2	2.9	3.4	3.8	4.4	4.9
53	25%	36%	39%	39%	38%	39%	39%	38%	36%
54	0.3	1.0	1.7	2.5	3.0	3.6	4.0	4.6	5.2
54	31%	39%	41%	39%	39%	39%	39%	39%	40%
55	0.5	1.5	2.3	3.2	3.8	4.3	4.9	5.5	6.2
55	37%	39%	39%	37%	37%	36%	36%	37%	34%
56	0.8	1.8	2.6	3.4	4.1	4.6	5.1	5.7	6.4
56	39%	40%	39%	39%	39%	39%	40%	38%	37%
57	1.2	2.4	3.3	4.3	5.0	5.6	6.1	6.7	7.3
57	39%	36%	35%	34%	35%	35%	35%	33%	35%
58	1.6	2.8	3.7	4.7	5.3	5.9	6.3	7.0	7.6
58	39%	40%	38%	37%	38%	39%	39%	40%	39%
59	2.2	3.6	4.5	5.5	6.2	6.8	7.3	7.9	8.5
59	38%	35%	36%	37%	38%	39%	39%	40%	39%
60	2.8	4.1	5.0	6.0	6.6	7.2	7.7	8.3	9.1
60	37%	38%	39%	42%	43%	41%	42%	42%	43%
61	3.5	4.9	5.8	6.8	7.5	8.2	8.7	9.4	10.
61	40%	40%	42%	41%	42%	41%	43%	42%	42%
62	4.3	5.6	6.5	7.5	8.2	8.8	9.3	10.	10.
62	42%	43%	43%	44%	44%	44%	42%	42%	42%
63	5.4	6.7	7.6	8.6	9.3	10.	10.	11.	11.
63	41%	43%	42%	41%	41%	40%	41%	40%	39%
64	6.3	7.6	8.4	9.4	10.	10.	11.	11.	12.
64	42%	40%	40%	40%	40%	40%	41%	42%	42%
65	7.3	8.6	9.5	10.	11.	11.	12.	12.	13.
65	40%	40%	40%	40%	40%	40%	41%	40%	38%

High Volatility

STOCK PRICE	NUMBER OF MONTHS BEFORE THE OPTIONS EXPIRE								
	1	2	3	4	5	6	7	8	9
45	0.0	0.6	1.2	2.1	2.7	3.3	3.8	4.6	5.5
45	6%	23%	27%	32%	32%	32%	33%	32%	32%
46	0.0	0.7	1.3	2.2	2.9	3.4	3.9	4.7	5.7
46	10%	25%	32%	32%	33%	35%	34%	34%	34%
47	0.1	0.8	1.6	2.6	3.4	4.1	4.7	5.6	6.6
47	12%	26%	33%	33%	32%	32%	33%	34%	33%
48	0.1	1.0	1.9	2.9	3.7	4.3	4.9	5.8	6.7
48	16%	30%	32%	32%	33%	33%	34%	34%	34%
49	0.2	1.2	2.2	3.4	4.2	5.0	5.7	6.6	7.6
49	21%	32%	32%	32%	32%	33%	33%	33%	35%
50	0.3	1.4	2.4	3.6	4.5	5.2	5.9	6.8	7.9
50	24%	32%	34%	34%	35%	34%	36%	35%	35%
51	0.5	1.8	2.9	4.3	5.2	6.0	6.7	7.7	8.7
51	25%	33%	34%	34%	35%	35%	36%	36%	36%
52	0.6	2.1	3.3	4.7	5.6	6.3	7.0	8.0	9.0
52	32%	34%	34%	35%	35%	35%	35%	36%	35%
53	0.9	2.6	3.9	5.4	6.3	7.1	7.9	8.8	10.
53	32%	32%	34%	35%	35%	35%	35%	34%	35%
54	1.1	2.9	4.2	5.7	6.7	7.5	8.1	9.1	10.
54	34%	36%	35%	37%	36%	36%	36%	37%	38%
55	1.6	3.6	5.1	6.5	7.6	8.4	9.1	10.	11.
55	33%	36%	35%	37%	36%	36%	37%	37%	38%
56	2.0	4.0	5.4	7.0	7.9	8.8	9.5	10.	11.
56	36%	35%	38%	38%	37%	37%	38%	40%	41%
57	2.6	4.9	6.3	7.9	9.0	9.8	10.	11.	12.
57	35%	37%	37%	36%	37%	37%	38%	38%	38%
58	3.1	5.3	6.8	8.4	9.4	10.	10.	12.	13.
58	37%	38%	37%	39%	40%	41%	41%	40%	37%
59	3.8	6.1	7.6	9.2	10.	11.	11.	13.	14.
59	38%	40%	39%	40%	40%	41%	41%	38%	37%
60	4.5	6.7	8.3	9.9	10.	11.	12.	13.	14.
60	40%	40%	40%	41%	40%	40%	41%	40%	40%
61	5.2	7.6	9.1	10.	11.	12.	13.	14.	15.
61	41%	40%	40%	40%	40%	40%	40%	40%	40%
62	6.0	8.3	9.8	11.	12.	13.	14.	15.	16.
62	41%	41%	41%	40%	40%	40%	40%	40%	40%
63	7.0	9.3	10.	12.	13.	14.	15.	16.	17.
63	42%	42%	42%	40%	40%	40%	40%	40%	40%
64	8.0	10.	11.	13.	14.	15.	15.	17.	18.
64	41%	42%	41%	40%	40%	40%	41%	41%	40%
65	9.0	11.	12.	14.	15.	16.	17.	18.	19.
65	41%	41%	41%	40%	40%	40%	40%	40%	40%

HIGH PRICE CALL TABLE

Exercise Price is (70)

Average Volatility

STOCK PRICE

NUMBER OF MONTHS BEFORE THE OPTIONS EXPIRE

	1	2	3	4	5	6	7	8	9
55	0.0	0.1	0.4	0.8	1.1	1.5	1.9	2.4	2.9
55	1%	11%	22%	27%	33%	34%	37%	38%	39%
56	0.0	0.1	0.4	0.8	1.2	1.6	1.9	2.4	3.0
56	1%	17%	24%	32%	36%	39%	39%	39%	39%
57	0.0	0.2	0.6	1.1	1.6	2.0	2.5	3.1	3.6
57	3%	19%	26%	33%	36%	38%	39%	39%	39%
58	0.0	0.2	0.7	1.3	1.8	2.2	2.6	3.2	3.8
58	4%	25%	32%	36%	39%	39%	39%	39%	40%
59	0.0	0.4	0.9	1.6	2.2	2.7	3.2	3.8	4.5
59	9%	25%	35%	39%	39%	39%	39%	39%	38%
60	0.0	0.5	1.1	1.7	2.3	2.9	3.4	4.0	4.5
60	13%	32%	39%	39%	39%	39%	39%	39%	40%
61	0.1	0.7	1.5	2.3	3.0	3.6	4.1	4.7	5.4
61	19%	35%	38%	39%	39%	39%	39%	38%	38%
62	0.2	0.9	1.6	2.5	3.1	3.7	4.2	4.9	5.6
62	25%	39%	40%	41%	40%	39%	39%	39%	40%
63	0.4	1.4	2.3	3.2	3.9	4.5	5.0	5.8	6.6
63	30%	38%	39%	38%	39%	38%	38%	37%	35%
64	0.5	1.6	2.5	3.4	4.1	4.7	5.3	6.0	6.7
64	38%	41%	39%	40%	39%	40%	40%	39%	37%
65	0.9	2.1	3.2	4.1	4.9	5.6	6.2	7.0	7.7
65	39%	39%	38%	36%	37%	36%	36%	34%	34%
66	1.1	2.4	3.4	4.4	5.2	5.8	6.4	7.1	7.8
66	41%	39%	39%	40%	38%	38%	38%	38%	40%
67	1.7	3.1	4.2	5.3	6.1	6.9	7.4	8.1	8.9
67	39%	36%	35%	35%	36%	34%	34%	36%	38%
68	2.0	3.5	4.6	5.7	6.5	7.1	7.7	8.4	9.2
68	39%	39%	36%	38%	40%	39%	40%	41%	40%
69	2.7	4.3	5.4	6.6	7.3	8.0	8.6	9.3	10.
69	36%	35%	35%	38%	39%	40%	39%	38%	39%
70	3.2	4.8	5.9	7.0	7.8	8.4	9.0	9.8	10.
70	37%	38%	40%	42%	43%	41%	42%	43%	43%
71	4.0	5.7	6.7	7.9	8.7	9.5	10.	10.	11.
71	40%	41%	42%	41%	42%	41%	44%	43%	42%
72	4.8	6.3	7.4	8.5	9.3	10.	10.	11.	12.
72	41%	43%	44%	44%	45%	45%	45%	43%	42%
73	5.8	7.3	8.4	9.6	10.	11.	11.	12.	13.
73	42%	43%	43%	41%	42%	41%	42%	41%	40%
74	6.7	8.2	9.3	10.	11.	11.	12.	13.	14.
74	43%	42%	41%	40%	41%	41%	41%	42%	42%
75	7.8	9.3	10.	11.	12.	13.	13.	14.	15.
75	41%	40%	40%	40%	40%	41%	40%	39%	40%

High Volatility

STOCK PRICE

NUMBER OF MONTHS BEFORE THE OPTIONS EXPIRE

	1	2	3	4	5	6	7	8	9
55	0.1	1.1	2.0	3.2	4.1	4.8	5.6	6.7	7.9
55	12%	25%	32%	32%	32%	33%	33%	33%	33%
56	0.2	1.2	2.1	3.4	4.3	5.0	5.8	6.8	7.9
56	15%	30%	32%	34%	34%	34%	34%	35%	35%
57	0.2	1.4	2.6	4.0	5.0	5.8	6.7	7.8	9.1
57	22%	33%	32%	32%	32%	34%	34%	34%	34%
58	0.3	1.7	2.9	4.3	5.2	6.1	6.9	7.9	9.2
58	23%	32%	33%	33%	34%	34%	36%	35%	35%
59	0.5	2.0	3.3	4.9	6.0	6.9	7.7	8.8	10.
59	25%	32%	32%	33%	34%	35%	35%	35%	35%
60	0.6	2.2	3.6	5.1	6.3	7.0	7.9	9.1	10.
60	30%	34%	34%	35%	35%	35%	35%	36%	36%
61	0.9	2.7	4.2	5.9	7.0	7.9	8.8	10.	11.
61	33%	33%	34%	35%	35%	36%	35%	35%	34%
62	1.0	3.1	4.6	6.2	7.4	8.2	9.1	10.	11.
62	33%	35%	34%	35%	36%	36%	36%	36%	37%
63	1.5	3.7	5.3	7.0	8.2	9.1	10.	11.	12.
63	33%	35%	35%	35%	36%	35%	34%	35%	37%
64	1.7	4.0	5.6	7.3	8.5	9.4	10.	11.	12.
64	35%	35%	35%	37%	38%	37%	37%	38%	38%
65	2.3	4.8	6.5	8.3	9.5	10.	11.	12.	14.
65	34%	35%	37%	37%	38%	37%	37%	38%	38%
66	2.7	5.2	6.9	8.6	9.8	10.	11.	12.	14.
66	36%	38%	39%	37%	37%	40%	39%	40%	40%
67	3.4	6.1	7.8	9.7	10.	11.	12.	14.	15.
67	34%	37%	38%	37%	37%	39%	39%	38%	38%
68	3.9	6.6	8.3	10.	11.	12.	13.	14.	15.
68	36%	40%	39%	40%	41%	40%	40%	40%	37%
69	4.6	7.4	9.1	11.	12.	13.	14.	15.	16.
69	38%	39%	40%	40%	40%	40%	40%	37%	38%
70	5.3	8.0	9.7	11.	12.	13.	14.	16.	17.
70	41%	40%	40%	40%	40%	41%	41%	41%	40%
71	6.0	8.8	10.	12.	13.	14.	15.	17.	18.
71	41%	40%	40%	40%	40%	40%	41%	40%	40%
72	6.8	9.5	11.	13.	14.	15.	16.	17.	19.
72	41%	41%	41%	40%	40%	40%	40%	40%	40%
73	7.8	10.	12.	14.	15.	16.	17.	18.	20.
73	41%	41%	41%	41%	40%	40%	40%	40%	40%
74	8.7	11.	13.	15.	16.	17.	18.	19.	21.
74	42%	42%	42%	41%	41%	40%	40%	40%	40%
75	9.8	12.	14.	16.	17.	18.	19.	20.	22.
75	41%	42%	41%	40%	40%	40%	40%	41%	40%

HIGH PRICE CALL TABLE

Exercise Price is (80)

Average Volatility

STOCK PRICE	NUMBER OF MONTHS BEFORE THE OPTIONS EXPIRE								
	1	2	3	4	5	6	7	8	9
65	0.0	0.3	0.7	1.3	1.9	2.4	2.9	3.5	4.2
65	4 %	20%	25%	32%	35%	38%	39%	39%	38%
66	0.0	0.3	0.8	1.4	1.9	2.4	2.9	3.5	4.2
66	4 %	22%	33%	36%	39%	39%	39%	39%	39%
67	0.0	0.4	1.0	1.8	2.4	3.0	3.6	4.2	5.0
67	6 %	25%	34%	36%	38%	39%	39%	39%	38%
68	0.0	0.5	1.2	1.9	2.6	3.2	3.7	4.3	5.1
68	10%	28%	36%	40%	39%	39%	39%	39%	40%
69	0.1	0.7	1.5	2.4	3.2	3.8	4.4	5.1	5.9
69	17%	32%	38%	38%	38%	39%	39%	39%	38%
70	0.2	0.9	1.7	2.6	3.3	4.0	4.5	5.1	5.9
70	21%	38%	39%	39%	39%	39%	39%	39%	39%
71	0.3	1.3	2.2	3.2	4.0	4.7	5.3	6.0	7.0
71	24%	38%	39%	38%	38%	38%	39%	38%	36%
72	0.4	1.4	2.3	3.4	4.2	4.9	5.4	6.2	7.2
72	32%	39%	40%	40%	39%	39%	39%	40%	37%
73	0.7	2.0	3.0	4.1	5.0	5.7	6.4	7.2	8.2
73	35%	38%	39%	38%	36%	36%	36%	36%	35%
74	0.8	2.2	3.2	4.3	5.2	6.0	6.6	7.4	8.3
74	39%	40%	39%	39%	39%	39%	39%	38%	36%
75	1.3	2.8	4.0	5.1	6.1	6.9	7.6	8.4	9.2
75	39%	38%	36%	36%	34%	34%	34%	35%	34%
76	1.5	3.1	4.2	5.4	6.3	7.1	7.7	8.4	9.4
76	41%	39%	39%	39%	39%	38%	38%	41%	39%
77	2.2	3.9	5.1	6.4	7.4	8.2	8.7	9.6	10.
77	38%	36%	35%	36%	35%	35%	36%	38%	38%
78	2.5	4.3	5.5	6.7	7.7	8.4	9.0	9.8	10.
78	42%	36%	36%	39%	38%	39%	40%	40%	38%
79	3.2	5.1	6.3	7.6	8.6	9.4	10.	10.	11.
79	36%	35%	37%	38%	39%	39%	39%	38%	39%
80	3.7	5.6	6.8	8.1	9.0	9.8	10.	11.	12.
80	37%	39%	40%	42%	42%	41%	43%	44%	45%
81	4.5	6.4	7.6	9.0	10.	10.	11.	12.	13.
81	40%	40%	41%	40%	41%	41%	43%	44%	42%
82	5.2	7.1	8.3	9.5	10.	11.	11.	12.	13.
82	40%	42%	43%	44%	44%	45%	45%	44%	42%
83	6.2	8.0	9.2	10.	11.	12.	13.	14.	15.
83	40%	42%	43%	43%	41%	41%	42%	42%	41%
84	7.2	8.9	10.	11.	12.	13.	13.	14.	15.
84	42%	44%	42%	42%	42%	42%	42%	42%	42%
85	8.2	10.	11.	12.	13.	14.	14.	15.	16.
85	·41%	40%	41%	40%	40%	40%	40%	41%	39%

High Volatility

STOCK PRICE	NUMBER OF MONTHS BEFORE THE OPTIONS EXPIRE								
	1	2	3	4	5	6	7	8	9
65	0.3	1.7	2.9	4.5	5.7	6.7	7.6	8.8	10.
65	21%	32%	33%	32%	33%	33%	34%	34%	35%
66	0.4	1.8	3.1	4.7	5.8	6.8	7.7	8.9	10.
66	24%	33%	35%	35%	35%	36%	37%	35%	35%
67	0.5	2.2	3.7	5.5	6.8	7.8	8.7	10.	11.
67	24%	32%	33%	33%	34%	34%	34%	35%	36%
68	0.7	2.5	4.0	5.7	7.0	7.9	8.8	10.	11.
68	26%	32%	34%	35%	35%	35%	35%	35%	35%
69	0.8	2.9	4.6	6.5	7.8	8.8	9.8	11.	12.
69	32%	32%	32%	35%	35%	35%	35%	35%	34%
70	1.0	3.1	4.8	6.7	8.0	9.0	10.	11.	12.
70	33%	35%	36%	35%	35%	37%	36%	37%	36%
71	1.3	3.7	5.6	7.5	8.9	10.	11.	12.	13.
71	33%	32%	35%	36%	35%	35%	36%	34%	36%
72	1.6	4.1	5.9	7.9	9.2	10.	11.	12.	14.
72	34%	35%	35%	37%	35%	36%	36%	37%	38%
73	2.1	4.7	6.7	8.7	10.	11.	12.	13.	15.
73	33%	35%	34%	36%	36%	35%	37%	37%	38%
74	2.4	5.1	7.0	9.0	10.	11.	12.	13.	15.
74	36%	36%	38%	38%	37%	38%	38%	38%	40%
75	3.0	5.9	7.9	10.	11.	12.	13.	15.	16.
75	35%	36%	37%	37%	37%	37%	39%	39%	38%
76	3.4	6.3	8.2	10.	11.	12.	13.	15.	16.
76	35%	37%	40%	38%	38%	39%	41%	40%	40%
77	4.2	7.3	9.3	11.	12.	14.	15.	16.	18.
77	34%	37%	37%	37%	38%	39%	38%	38%	37%
78	4.7	7.7	9.7	11.	13.	14.	15.	16.	18.
78	38%	40%	40%	40%	41%	40%	40%	39%	38%
79	5.4	8.5	10.	12.	14.	15.	16.	18.	19.
79	39%	41%	41%	40%	40%	41%	40%	37%	39%
80	6.1	9.2	11.	13.	14.	15.	16.	18.	20.
80	40%	40%	40%	40%	40%	40%	40%	40%	40%
81	6.8	10.	12.	14.	15.	16.	17.	19.	21.
81	40%	40%	40%	40%	40%	40%	40%	40%	40%
82	7.6	10.	12.	14.	16.	17.	18.	20.	21.
82	41%	41%	41%	40%	40%	40%	40%	40%	40%
83	8.6	11.	13.	15.	17.	18.	19.	21.	22.
83	42%	41%	41%	41%	40%	41%	41%	41%	40%
84	9.5	12.	14.	16.	18.	19.	20.	21.	23.
84	41%	41%	41%	41%	40%	40%	41%	40%	40%
85	10.	13.	15.	17.	19.	20.	21.	23.	25.
85	41%	41%	41%	40%	40%	40%	40%	40%	40%

HIGH PRICE CALL TABLE
Exercise Price is ⑨⓪

Average Volatility

STOCK PRICE — NUMBER OF MONTHS BEFORE THE OPTIONS EXPIRE

STOCK PRICE	1	2	3	4	5	6	7	8	9
75	0.0	0.3	0.9	1.8	2.5	3.2	3.8	4.6	5.4
75	3%	23%	30%	38%	39%	40%	40%	42%	41%
76	0.0	0.6	1.4	2.3	3.2	3.8	4.5	5.4	6.3
76	6%	24%	28%	34%	36%	38%	38%	38%	36%
77	0.0	0.6	1.4	2.4	3.2	3.9	4.6	5.3	6.2
77	9%	27%	39%	41%	42%	42%	42%	42%	42%
78	0.1	0.9	1.9	3.0	4.0	4.8	5.4	6.3	7.1
78	13%	28%	35%	37%	39%	38%	39%	36%	37%
79	0.1	1.0	2.0	3.2	4.1	4.8	5.5	6.3	7.2
79	18%	39%	41%	42%	41%	41%	42%	42%	41%
80	0.3	1.6	2.7	3.9	4.9	5.7	6.4	7.1	8.1
80	25%	36%	39%	38%	38%	37%	36%	37%	33%
81	0.4	1.6	2.7	4.0	4.9	5.7	6.3	7.2	8.2
81	27%	43%	44%	42%	42%	42%	43%	42%	39%
82	0.7	2.3	3.5	4.8	5.9	6.5	7.3	8.2	9.3
82	33%	40%	40%	36%	33%	36%	33%	35%	34%
83	0.9	2.5	3.7	5.0	6.0	6.8	7.5	8.4	9.4
83	40%	42%	43%	40%	40%	38%	38%	38%	36%
84	1.3	3.1	4.5	5.8	6.9	7.8	8.5	9.4	10.
84	39%	41%	37%	33%	34%	33%	35%	35%	38%
85	1.6	3.4	4.7	6.0	7.1	7.9	8.6	9.5	10.
85	44%	42%	42%	37%	36%	37%	38%	39%	40%
86	2.2	4.1	5.5	7.0	8.1	9.0	9.7	10.	11.
86	41%	33%	34%	35%	36%	36%	38%	37%	37%
87	2.5	4.4	5.8	7.2	8.3	9.1	9.8	10.	11.
87	44%	40%	36%	39%	41%	41%	41%	42%	42%
88	3.1	5.2	6.7	8.1	9.3	10.	11.	11.	13.
88	34%	34%	36%	38%	40%	40%	40%	41%	43%
89	3.6	5.7	7.2	8.6	9.7	10.	11.	12.	13.
89	36%	39%	41%	42%	43%	42%	43%	43%	44%
90	4.4	6.6	8.1	9.6	10.	11.	12.	13.	14.
90	34%	40%	41%	42%	42%	41%	40%	41%	42%
91	5.0	7.2	8.6	10.	11.	12.	12.	13.	15.
91	38%	43%	44%	44%	41%	44%	47%	49%	49%
92	6.0	8.1	9.7	11.	12.	13.	14.	15.	16.
92	43%	43%	43%	40%	42%	42%	43%	46%	44%
93	6.8	8.9	10.	11.	12.	13.	14.	15.	16.
93	43%	44%	42%	43%	45%	45%	46%	44%	43%
94	7.9	10.	11.	12.	14.	15.	15.	16.	18.
94	43%	41%	41%	40%	41%	40%	41%	42%	41%
95	8.8	10.	12.	13.	14.	15.	16.	17.	18.
95	43%	43%	41%	41%	41%	41%	41%	41%	42%

High Volatility

STOCK PRICE — NUMBER OF MONTHS BEFORE THE OPTIONS EXPIRE

STOCK PRICE	1	2	3	4	5	6	7	8	9
75	0.4	2.3	4.1	6.1	7.5	8.6	9.5	11.	12.
75	19%	33%	35%	32%	32%	33%	34%	36%	35%
76	0.7	2.8	4.7	6.8	8.3	9.3	10.	12.	13.
76	24%	31%	32%	33%	31%	33%	34%	34%	33%
77	0.8	3.0	4.9	7.0	8.5	9.6	10.	12.	13.
77	27%	35%	35%	33%	34%	35%	36%	36%	36%
78	1.1	3.6	5.7	7.9	9.3	10.	11.	13.	15.
78	29%	31%	32%	31%	33%	35%	35%	33%	35%
79	1.2	3.9	5.9	8.1	9.7	10.	11.	13.	15.
79	35%	35%	32%	33%	35%	35%	38%	36%	37%
80	1.6	4.5	6.7	8.9	10.	11.	12.	14.	16.
80	34%	32%	31%	32%	35%	35%	37%	36%	33%
81	1.8	4.8	6.9	9.2	10.	12.	13.	14.	16.
81	37%	35%	34%	35%	37%	37%	39%	37%	36%
82	2.4	5.5	7.8	10.	11.	13.	14.	15.	17.
82	35%	32%	31%	37%	35%	35%	35%	34%	36%
83	2.7	5.9	8.1	10.	12.	13.	14.	16.	17.
83	36%	33%	36%	38%	40%	37%	35%	39%	38%
84	3.3	6.7	9.0	11.	13.	14.	15.	17.	19.
84	33%	33%	35%	37%	36%	35%	35%	38%	38%
85	3.7	7.0	9.3	11.	13.	14.	15.	17.	19.
85	36%	36%	39%	37%	35%	36%	39%	39%	40%
86	4.4	8.0	10.	12.	14.	15.	17.	18.	20.
86	33%	35%	39%	34%	35%	35%	38%	37%	38%
87	4.8	8.4	10.	13.	14.	16.	17.	19.	20.
87	35%	40%	41%	37%	38%	40%	40%	40%	40%
88	5.6	9.2	11.	14.	15.	17.	18.	20.	22.
88	34%	40%	35%	37%	38%	38%	40%	40%	37%
89	6.2	9.9	12.	14.	16.	17.	18.	20.	22.
89	38%	42%	37%	40%	42%	41%	42%	40%	35%
90	7.1	10.	13.	15.	17.	18.	20.	22.	23.
90	42%	36%	37%	39%	40%	40%	40%	36%	35%
91	7.8	11.	13.	16.	18.	19.	20.	22.	24.
91	43%	41%	42%	42%	42%	41%	38%	36%	37%
92	8.7	12.	14.	17.	19.	20.	21.	23.	25.
92	43%	41%	42%	42%	40%	37%	37%	35%	35%
93	9.6	13.	15.	18.	19.	21.	22.	24.	26.
93	43%	43%	43%	43%	41%	38%	40%	40%	39%
94	10.	14.	16.	19.	21.	22.	23.	25.	27.
94	43%	43%	43%	40%	37%	37%	38%	38%	39%
95	11.	15.	17.	20.	21.	22.	24.	25.	27.
95	43%	43%	43%	40%	41%	41%	42%	42%	42%

HIGH PRICE CALL TABLE

Exercise Price is (100)

Average Volatility

STOCK PRICE	NUMBER OF MONTHS BEFORE THE OPTIONS EXPIRE								
	1	2	3	4	5	6	7	8	9
85	0.0	0.6	1.5	2.5	3.4	4.2	4.9	5.8	6.7
85	8%	27%	38%	40%	42%	42%	42%	42%	42%
86	0.1	1.0	2.0	3.1	4.1	5.0	5.7	6.8	7.5
86	9%	27%	33%	36%	39%	37%	40%	36%	38%
87	0.1	1.0	2.1	3.2	4.2	5.0	5.7	6.7	7.5
87	15%	35%	40%	42%	41%	42%	42%	42%	42%
88	0.2	1.5	2.6	3.9	5.1	5.9	6.6	7.5	8.7
88	18%	33%	38%	38%	37%	37%	38%	37%	33%
89	0.3	1.5	2.8	4.1	5.2	6.0	6.6	7.7	8.7
89	26%	41%	42%	41%	41%	42%	43%	41%	38%
90	0.6	2.2	3.4	4.9	6.0	6.9	7.5	8.6	9.7
90	27%	36%	40%	38%	36%	34%	37%	33%	33%
91	0.7	2.2	3.5	4.9	6.0	6.8	7.6	8.6	9.7
91	37%	44%	42%	42%	41%	42%	43%	41%	37%
92	1.1	2.9	4.3	5.8	6.9	7.8	8.6	9.7	10.
92	37%	40%	38%	35%	35%	34%	34%	33%	35%
93	1.3	3.1	4.6	6.0	7.1	8.1	8.7	9.9	11.
93	41%	42%	42%	40%	39%	37%	38%	37%	39%
94	1.8	3.8	5.3	6.8	8.1	9.0	9.8	11.	12.
94	41%	39%	33%	33%	33%	35%	35%	38%	37%
95	2.0	4.1	5.6	7.0	8.2	9.2	9.9	11.	12.
95	43%	42%	38%	37%	36%	37%	39%	39%	40%
96	2.7	4.9	6.4	8.0	9.3	10.	11.	12.	13.
96	41%	32%	33%	36%	35%	37%	37%	38%	38%
97	3.0	5.2	6.7	8.2	9.5	10.	11.	12.	13.
97	43%	38%	36%	40%	43%	42%	42%	42%	42%
98	3.7	6.0	7.6	9.2	10.	11.	12.	13.	14.
98	36%	34%	36%	41%	41%	41%	41%	42%	41%
99	4.2	6.4	8.1	9.7	10.	11.	12.	13.	15.
99	36%	39%	41%	42%	42%	43%	45%	42%	44%
100	5.0	7.4	9.0	10.	12.	13.	13.	15.	16.
100	35%	40%	41%	41%	42%	41%	41%	41%	42%
101	5.5	7.9	9.5	11.	12.	13.	14.	15.	16.
101	35%	41%	44%	44%	41%	44%	47%	49%	49%
102	6.5	8.9	10.	12.	13.	14.	15.	16.	18.
102	42%	43%	43%	42%	41%	42%	46%	46%	44%
103	7.3	9.6	11.	12.	14.	15.	15.	17.	18.
103	43%	44%	42%	43%	45%	46%	46%	45%	44%
104	8.4	10.	12.	13.	15.	16.	17.	18.	19.
104	43%	43%	41%	41%	42%	41%	44%	41%	41%
105	9.3	11.	13.	14.	16.	16.	17.	18.	20.
105	43%	43%	41%	41%	41%	41%	41%	41%	41%

High Volatility

STOCK PRICE	NUMBER OF MONTHS BEFORE THE OPTIONS EXPIRE								
	1	2	3	4	5	6	7	8	9
85	0.8	3.2	5.3	7.6	9.2	10.	11.	13.	15.
85	26%	33%	34%	33%	33%	34%	36%	35%	37%
86	1.1	3.8	5.9	8.3	10.	11.	12.	14.	16.
86	26%	31%	32%	31%	33%	34%	35%	34%	35%
87	1.2	4.0	6.2	8.6	10.	11.	12.	14.	16.
87	31%	34%	34%	34%	37%	35%	36%	36%	38%
88	1.6	4.7	7.0	9.4	11.	12.	13.	15.	17.
88	31%	32%	33%	33%	34%	35%	34%	35%	33%
89	1.8	5.0	7.3	9.7	11.	12.	14.	15.	17.
89	35%	34%	35%	36%	36%	35%	37%	38%	35%
90	2.3	5.6	8.0	10.	12.	13.	15.	16.	19.
90	35%	32%	32%	35%	34%	35%	34%	35%	34%
91	2.5	5.9	8.3	10.	12.	14.	15.	17.	19.
91	37%	34%	33%	37%	37%	39%	37%	35%	39%
92	3.1	6.8	9.2	11.	13.	15.	16.	18.	20.
92	35%	33%	34%	35%	36%	35%	35%	35%	36%
93	3.5	7.1	9.5	12.	14.	15.	16.	18.	20.
93	36%	34%	37%	40%	37%	35%	37%	38%	39%
94	4.1	7.9	10.	13.	15.	16.	17.	19.	21.
94	34%	32%	37%	39%	34%	35%	35%	38%	37%
95	4.5	8.2	10.	13.	15.	16.	18.	19.	22.
95	34%	35%	40%	38%	35%	38%	39%	40%	40%
96	5.3	9.2	11.	14.	16.	18.	19.	21.	23.
96	31%	35%	40%	35%	35%	35%	38%	39%	38%
97	5.7	9.6	12.	14.	16.	18.	19.	21.	23.
97	36%	40%	37%	38%	39%	40%	41%	41%	40%
98	6.5	10.	13.	16.	17.	19.	20.	22.	24.
98	35%	41%	35%	38%	38%	38%	40%	40%	36%
99	7.1	11.	13.	16.	18.	20.	21.	23.	25.
99	38%	41%	38%	42%	42%	41%	42%	40%	35%
100	8.0	12.	14.	17.	19.	21.	22.	24.	26.
100	41%	36%	39%	40%	40%	40%	40%	36%	35%
101	8.6	12.	15.	18.	20.	21.	22.	24.	27.
101	43%	41%	42%	42%	42%	41%	38%	36%	37%
102	9.6	13.	16.	19.	21.	22.	24.	26.	28.
102	43%	41%	42%	42%	40%	37%	36%	35%	35%
103	10.	14.	17.	19.	21.	23.	24.	26.	28.
103	43%	43%	43%	43%	41%	38%	40%	39%	39%
104	11.	15.	18.	21.	23.	24.	25.	27.	30.
104	42%	43%	43%	43%	37%	36%	37%	38%	39%
105	12.	16.	18.	21.	23.	25.	26.	28.	30.
105	43%	43%	43%	42%	40%	40%	43%	42%	42%

HIGH PRICE PUT TABLE
Exercise Price is (15)

Average Volatility

STOCK PRICE — NUMBER OF MONTHS BEFORE THE OPTIONS EXPIRE

STOCK PRICE	1	2	3	4	5	6	7	8	9
20	0.0	0.0	0.0	0.0	0.0	0.0	0.0	0.0	0.0
20	1 %	1 %	1 %	1 %	1 %	1 %	1 %	1 %	1 %
19	0.0	0.0	0.0	0.0	0.0	0.0	0.0	0.0	0.0
19	1 %	1 %	1 %	1 %	1 %	1 %	1 %	1 %	1 %
18	0.0	0.0	0.0	0.0	0.0	0.0	0.0	0.0	0.0
18	1 %	1 %	1 %	1 %	1 %	1 %	1 %	1 %	1 %
17	0.0	0.0	0.0	0.0	0.0	0.0	0.0	0.0	0.0
17	1 %	1 %	1 %	1 %	1 %	1 %	1 %	1 %	1 %
16	0.0	0.0	0.0	0.0	0.0	0.0	0.0	0.0	0.0
16	1 %	1 %	1 %	1 %	1 %	1 %	1 %	1 %	1 %
15	0.0	0.0	0.0	0.0	0.0	0.0	0.0	0.0	0.0
15	1 %	1 %	1 %	1 %	1 %	1 %	0 %	2 %	3 %
14	0.0	0.0	0.0	0.0	0.0	0.0	0.0	0.0	0.0
14	1 %	1 %	1 %	0 %	4 %	4 %	6 %	7 %	13%
13	0.0	0.0	0.0	0.0	0.0	0.1	0.0	0.0	0.1
13	1 %	1 %	4 %	8 %	12%	18%	21%	25%	27%
12	0.0	0.0	0.0	0.0	0.1	0.1	0.2	0.2	0.3
12	1 %	8 %	21%	27%	34%	39%	38%	39%	39%
11	0.0	0.0	0.1	0.2	0.3	0.4	0.5	0.5	0.6
11	26%	39%	41%	41%	39%	41%	39%	40%	40%
10	0.3	0.5	0.5	0.7	0.8	0.9	0.9	1.0	1.1
10	35%	36%	38%	38%	41%	41%	41%	40%	39%
9	1.2	1.3	1.4	1.5	1.6	1.6	1.7	1.7	1.9
9	26%	39%	41%	41%	39%	41%	39%	40%	40%
8	2.2	2.2	2.3	2.4	2.5	2.6	2.6	2.6	2.7
8	1 %	8 %	21%	27%	34%	39%	38%	39%	39%
7	3.1	3.2	3.3	3.4	3.5	3.5	3.5	3.6	3.7
7	1 %	1 %	4 %	8 %	12%	18%	21%	25%	27%
6	4.1	4.2	4.3	4.4	4.4	4.5	4.5	4.6	4.6
6	1 %	1 %	1 %	0 %	4 %	4 %	6 %	7 %	13%
5	5.1	5.2	5.2	5.3	5.4	5.4	5.5	5.5	5.5
5	1 %	1 %	1 %	1 %	1 %	1 %	0 %	2 %	3 %

High Volatility

STOCK PRICE — NUMBER OF MONTHS BEFORE THE OPTIONS EXPIRE

STOCK PRICE	1	2	3	4	5	6	7	8	9
20	0.0	0.0	0.0	0.0	0.0	0.0	0.0	0.0	0.0
20	1 %	1 %	1 %	1 %	1 %	1 %	1 %	1 %	1 %
19	0.0	0.0	0.0	0.0	0.0	0.0	0.0	0.0	0.0
19	1 %	1 %	1 %	1 %	1 %	1 %	1 %	1 %	0 %
18	0.0	0.0	0.0	0.0	0.0	0.0	0.0	0.0	0.0
18	1 %	1 %	1 %	1 %	1 %	1 %	1 %	1 %	1 %
17	0.0	0.0	0.0	0.0	0.0	0.0	0.0	0.0	0.0
17	1 %	1 %	1 %	1 %	0 %	1 %	1 %	2 %	2 %
16	0.0	0.0	0.0	0.0	0.0	0.0	0.0	0.0	0.0
16	1 %	1 %	1 %	1 %	1 %	2 %	3 %	7 %	9 %
15	0.0	0.0	0.0	0.0	0.0	0.0	0.0	0.0	0.1
15	1 %	1 %	1 %	2 %	5 %	9 %	9 %	13%	16%
14	0.0	0.0	0.0	0.0	0.0	0.0	0.1	0.1	0.2
14	1 %	1 %	4 %	9 %	13%	17%	19%	24%	25%
13	0.0	0.0	0.0	0.1	0.2	0.2	0.3	0.3	0.5
13	1 %	8 %	14%	23%	25%	28%	32%	37%	34%
12	0.0	0.1	0.2	0.3	0.4	0.5	0.6	0.7	0.9
12	9 %	24%	33%	36%	35%	35%	38%	38%	35%
11	0.0	0.3	0.4	0.6	0.8	0.9	1.0	1.1	1.3
11	38%	38%	38%	36%	33%	36%	35%	40%	36%
10	0.5	0.8	0.9	1.1	1.3	1.4	1.5	1.6	1.7
10	39%	41%	39%	41%	40%	40%	40%	42%	41%
9	1.3	1.6	1.7	1.9	2.0	2.2	2.3	2.3	2.5
9	38%	38%	38%	36%	33%	36%	35%	40%	36%
8	2.3	2.5	2.6	2.8	2.9	3.0	3.0	3.2	3.3
8	9 %	24%	33%	36%	35%	35%	38%	38%	35%
7	3.2	3.5	3.5	3.7	3.8	3.9	4.0	4.0	4.2
7	1 %	8 %	14%	23%	25%	28%	32%	37%	34%
6	4.2	4.4	4.5	4.6	4.7	4.8	4.9	4.9	5.1
6	1 %	1 %	4 %	9 %	13%	17%	19%	24%	25%
5	5.2	5.3	5.4	5.5	5.6	5.7	5.8	5.8	5.9
5	1 %	1 %	1 %	2 %	5 %	9 %	9 %	13%	16%

HIGH PRICE PUT TABLE

Exercise Price is ⑮

Average Volatility

STOCK PRICE — NUMBER OF MONTHS BEFORE THE OPTIONS EXPIRE

STOCK PRICE	1	2	3	4	5	6	7	8	9
25	0.0	0.0	0.0	0.0	0.0	0.0	0.0	0.0	0.0
25	1 %	1 %	1 %	1 %	1 %	1 %	1 %	1 %	1 %
24	0.0	0.0	0.0	0.0	0.0	0.0	0.0	0.0	0.0
24	1 %	1 %	1 %	1 %	1 %	1 %	1 %	1 %	1 %
23	0.0	0.0	0.0	0.0	0.0	0.0	0.0	0.0	0.0
23	1 %	1 %	1 %	1 %	1 %	1 %	0 %	1 %	4 %
22	0.0	0.0	0.0	0.0	0.0	0.0	0.0	0.0	0.0
22	1 %	1 %	1 %	1 %	1 %	1 %	4 %	4 %	7 %
21	0.0	0.0	0.0	0.0	0.0	0.0	0.0	0.0	0.0
21	1 %	1 %	1 %	1 %	4 %	4 %	8 %	10%	17%
20	0.0	0.0	0.0	0.0	0.0	0.0	0.0	0.0	0.1
20	1 %	1 %	1 %	4 %	9 %	14%	20%	21%	24%
19	0.0	0.0	0.0	0.0	0.0	0.1	0.1	0.2	0.2
19	1 %	4 %	8 %	17%	22%	26%	28%	34%	37%
18	0.0	0.0	0.0	0.1	0.2	0.3	0.3	0.4	0.5
18	1 %	12%	23%	30%	37%	38%	38%	39%	39%
17	0.0	0.0	0.1	0.3	0.4	0.5	0.6	0.7	0.9
17	15%	35%	39%	39%	39%	40%	40%	39%	39%
16	0.0	0.3	0.5	0.7	0.9	0.9	1.0	1.1	1.3
16	40%	40%	39%	39%	39%	40%	38%	37%	36%
15	0.5	0.7	1.0	1.1	1.3	1.4	1.5	1.7	1.7
15	36%	38%	38%	39%	41%	40%	41%	39%	40%
14	1.3	1.6	1.7	2.0	2.1	2.2	2.3	2.4	2.5
14	40%	40%	39%	39%	39%	40%	38%	37%	36%
13	2.3	2.5	2.7	2.8	2.9	3.1	3.1	3.2	3.3
13	15%	35%	39%	39%	39%	40%	40%	39%	39%
12	3.3	3.4	3.6	3.7	3.8	3.9	4.0	4.1	4.2
12	1 %	12%	23%	30%	37%	38%	38%	39%	39%
11	4.3	4.4	4.6	4.7	4.8	4.9	4.9	5.1	5.2
11	1 %	4 %	8 %	17%	22%	26%	28%	34%	37%
10	5.2	5.4	5.5	5.6	5.7	5.8	5.9	6.0	6.1
10	1 %	1 %	1 %	4 %	9 %	14%	20%	21%	24%

High Volatility

STOCK PRICE — NUMBER OF MONTHS BEFORE THE OPTIONS EXPIRE

STOCK PRICE	1	2	3	4	5	6	7	8	9
25	0.0	0.0	0.0	0.0	0.0	0.0	0.0	0.0	0.0
25	1 %	1 %	1 %	1 %	1 %	2 %	2 %	5 %	8 %
24	0.0	0.0	0.0	0.0	0.0	0.0	0.0	0.0	0.1
24	1 %	1 %	1 %	1 %	2 %	3 %	7 %	8 %	11%
23	0.0	0.0	0.0	0.0	0.0	0.0	0.0	0.1	0.1
23	1 %	1 %	1 %	2 %	6 %	9 %	9 %	12%	14%
22	0.0	0.0	0.0	0.0	0.0	0.0	0.1	0.2	0.3
22	1 %	1 %	2 %	7 %	10%	12%	14%	19%	21%
21	0.0	0.0	0.0	0.0	0.1	0.1	0.2	0.3	0.4
21	1 %	2 %	7 %	12%	17%	19%	24%	26%	29%
20	0.0	0.0	0.0	0.1	0.2	0.3	0.4	0.5	0.7
20	1 %	7 %	12%	19%	24%	27%	29%	30%	34%
19	0.0	0.0	0.1	0.3	0.4	0.5	0.7	0.8	1.0
19	2 %	13%	23%	29%	35%	36%	37%	38%	36%
18	0.0	0.1	0.3	0.6	0.8	0.9	1.1	1.3	1.5
18	10%	26%	35%	35%	36%	36%	36%	36%	36%
17	0.0	0.3	0.6	0.9	1.2	1.3	1.5	1.7	2.0
17	26%	36%	35%	35%	33%	33%	35%	36%	37%
16	0.3	0.8	1.0	1.4	1.6	1.8	1.9	2.1	2.4
16	38%	34%	37%	39%	40%	40%	38%	37%	38%
15	0.8	1.3	1.6	1.9	2.1	2.2	2.4	2.7	2.9
15	42%	42%	39%	43%	42%	41%	41%	41%	40%
14	1.7	2.1	2.4	2.7	2.9	3.0	3.2	3.4	3.6
14	38%	34%	37%	39%	40%	40%	38%	37%	38%
13	2.6	3.0	3.2	3.5	3.7	3.8	3.9	4.2	4.4
13	26%	36%	35%	35%	33%	33%	35%	36%	37%
12	3.6	3.9	4.1	4.4	4.6	4.7	4.8	5.0	5.2
12	10%	26%	35%	35%	36%	36%	36%	36%	36%
11	4.5	4.8	5.1	5.3	5.4	5.6	5.7	5.9	6.1
11	2 %	13%	23%	29%	35%	36%	37%	38%	36%
10	5.5	5.7	6.0	6.2	6.4	6.5	6.6	6.8	6.9
10	1 %	7 %	12%	19%	24%	27%	29%	30%	34%

HIGH PRICE PUT TABLE

Exercise Price is ⑳

Average Volatility

STOCK PRICE — NUMBER OF MONTHS BEFORE THE OPTIONS EXPIRE

STOCK PRICE	1	2	3	4	5	6	7	8	9
30	0.0	0.0	0.0	0.0	0.0	0.0	0.0	0.0	0.0
30	1 %	1 %	1 %	1 %	1 %	1 %	4 %	4 %	5 %
29	0.0	0.0	0.0	0.0	0.0	0.0	0.0	0.0	0.0
29	1 %	1 %	1 %	1 %	1 %	4 %	4 %	6 %	9 %
28	0.0	0.0	0.0	0.0	0.0	0.0	0.0	0.0	0.0
28	1 %	1 %	1 %	1 %	4 %	7 %	8 %	11%	17%
27	0.0	0.0	0.0	0.0	0.0	0.0	0.0	0.1	0.1
27	1 %	1 %	1 %	4 %	8 %	12%	17%	20%	24%
26	0.0	0.0	0.0	0.0	0.0	0.0	0.1	0.1	0.2
26	1 %	1 %	4 %	8 %	18%	22%	24%	27%	32%
25	0.0	0.0	0.0	0.0	0.1	0.2	0.3	0.4	0.5
25	1 %	4 %	12%	21%	25%	28%	34%	35%	37%
24	0.0	0.0	0.0	0.2	0.3	0.4	0.5	0.6	0.8
24	1 %	13%	25%	32%	37%	39%	39%	40%	40%
23	0.0	0.0	0.1	0.3	0.5	0.6	0.8	0.9	1.1
23	8 %	26%	37%	39%	39%	39%	41%	39%	39%
22	0.0	0.2	0.4	0.7	0.9	1.1	1.2	1.4	1.5
22	30%	39%	39%	39%	39%	39%	39%	40%	39%
21	0.2	0.6	0.8	1.1	1.3	1.5	1.6	1.8	2.0
21	40%	39%	40%	37%	36%	37%	35%	35%	36%
20	0.7	1.1	1.3	1.6	1.8	2.0	2.1	2.2	2.5
20	36%	37%	38%	40%	41%	41%	39%	40%	41%
19	1.5	1.9	2.2	2.4	2.6	2.7	2.9	3.0	3.2
19	40%	39%	40%	37%	36%	37%	35%	35%	36%
18	2.5	2.8	3.0	3.2	3.4	3.5	3.6	3.8	3.9
18	30%	39%	39%	39%	39%	39%	39%	40%	39%
17	3.5	3.7	3.9	4.1	4.3	4.4	4.5	4.7	4.8
17	8 %	26%	37%	39%	39%	39%	41%	39%	39%
16	4.4	4.7	4.8	5.0	5.2	5.3	5.4	5.6	5.7
16	1 %	13%	25%	32%	37%	39%	39%	40%	40%
15	5.4	5.7	5.8	6.0	6.2	6.3	6.4	6.5	6.7
15	1 %	4 %	12%	21%	25%	28%	34%	35%	37%

High Volatility

STOCK PRICE — NUMBER OF MONTHS BEFORE THE OPTIONS EXPIRE

STOCK PRICE	1	2	3	4	5	6	7	8	9
30	0.0	0.0	0.0	0.0	0.0	0.1	0.1	0.2	0.3
30	1 %	1 %	2 %	6 %	9 %	12%	13%	17%	19%
29	0.0	0.0	0.0	0.0	0.1	0.2	0.2	0.3	0.6
29	1 %	1 %	3 %	10%	11%	14%	18%	20%	23%
28	0.0	0.0	0.0	0.1	0.2	0.3	0.4	0.5	0.8
28	1 %	2 %	8 %	12%	17%	19%	23%	25%	30%
27	0.0	0.0	0.0	0.2	0.3	0.4	0.6	0.8	1.1
27	1 %	6 %	11%	19%	22%	25%	28%	29%	31%
26	0.0	0.0	0.1	0.3	0.5	0.6	0.8	1.1	1.3
26	1 %	11%	19%	26%	29%	34%	35%	36%	35%
25	0.0	0.1	0.3	0.6	0.8	1.0	1.1	1.4	1.8
25	3 %	19%	25%	31%	35%	35%	37%	37%	35%
24	0.0	0.2	0.5	0.8	1.1	1.3	1.5	1.8	2.1
24	12%	28%	35%	36%	37%	36%	38%	36%	33%
23	0.0	0.4	0.8	1.2	1.5	1.8	2.0	2.3	2.6
23	23%	35%	35%	36%	32%	34%	33%	37%	35%
22	0.2	0.8	1.3	1.6	1.9	2.2	2.4	2.7	3.0
22	36%	36%	34%	37%	35%	37%	37%	40%	37%
21	0.7	1.3	1.7	2.2	2.4	2.7	2.9	3.2	3.5
21	37%	37%	39%	40%	35%	35%	38%	40%	41%
20	1.1	1.8	2.2	2.7	2.9	3.2	3.4	3.7	4.0
20	42%	40%	40%	42%	42%	42%	42%	40%	37%
19	2.0	2.6	3.0	3.4	3.7	3.9	4.1	4.3	4.7
19	37%	37%	39%	40%	35%	35%	38%	40%	41%
18	2.9	3.5	3.8	4.2	4.5	4.7	4.9	5.1	5.5
18	36%	36%	34%	37%	35%	37%	37%	40%	37%
17	3.9	4.4	4.7	5.1	5.3	5.6	5.7	5.9	6.3
17	23%	35%	35%	36%	32%	34%	33%	37%	35%
16	4.8	5.3	5.6	5.9	6.2	6.4	6.5	6.7	7.1
16	12%	28%	35%	36%	37%	36%	38%	36%	33%
15	5.8	6.2	6.5	6.9	7.1	7.2	7.4	7.6	7.9
15	3 %	19%	25%	31%	35%	35%	37%	37%	35%

159

HIGH PRICE PUT TABLE
Exercise Price is (25)

Average Volatility

STOCK PRICE — NUMBER OF MONTHS BEFORE THE OPTIONS EXPIRE

STOCK PRICE	1	2	3	4	5	6	7	8	9
35	0.0	0.0	0.0	0.0	0.0	0.0	0.0	0.0	0.1
35	1 %	1 %	1 %	3 %	4 %	7 %	9 %	12%	19%
34	0.0	0.0	0.0	0.0	0.0	0.0	0.0	0.1	0.2
34	1 %	1 %	1 %	4 %	8 %	10%	16%	20%	23%
33	0.0	0.0	0.0	0.0	0.0	0.1	0.1	0.2	0.3
33	1 %	1 %	4 %	8 %	14%	20%	22%	24%	26%
32	0.0	0.0	0.0	0.0	0.1	0.1	0.2	0.3	0.5
32	1 %	4 %	6 %	17%	21%	24%	26%	31%	35%
31	0.0	0.0	0.0	0.1	0.2	0.3	0.4	0.5	0.7
31	1 %	5 %	18%	24%	29%	33%	37%	38%	39%
30	0.0	0.0	0.1	0.3	0.4	0.5	0.7	0.9	1.1
30	1 %	16%	24%	32%	35%	37%	39%	39%	39%
29	0.0	0.0	0.1	0.4	0.6	0.8	0.9	1.1	1.4
29	7 %	24%	35%	39%	39%	39%	39%	39%	40%
28	0.0	0.2	0.4	0.7	1.0	1.2	1.4	1.6	1.8
28	22%	38%	40%	40%	40%	39%	39%	39%	39%
27	0.1	0.5	0.8	1.1	1.4	1.6	1.8	2.0	2.2
27	39%	39%	39%	38%	38%	39%	38%	37%	35%
26	0.5	0.9	1.3	1.5	1.8	2.1	2.2	2.4	2.7
26	39%	38%	36%	35%	37%	35%	35%	37%	38%
25	0.9	1.4	1.7	2.1	2.3	2.5	2.7	2.9	3.2
25	36%	38%	38%	40%	43%	40%	39%	40%	41%
24	1.8	2.2	2.5	2.8	3.1	3.2	3.5	3.7	4.0
24	39%	38%	36%	35%	37%	35%	35%	37%	38%
23	2.7	3.1	3.4	3.7	3.9	4.1	4.3	4.5	4.7
23	39%	39%	39%	38%	38%	39%	38%	37%	35%
22	3.6	4.0	4.3	4.5	4.7	4.9	5.0	5.3	5.5
22	22%	38%	40%	40%	40%	39%	39%	39%	39%
21	4.6	4.9	5.2	5.4	5.7	5.8	5.9	6.2	6.4
21	7 %	24%	35%	39%	39%	39%	39%	39%	40%
20	5.6	5.9	6.1	6.4	6.6	6.7	6.9	7.0	7.3
20	1 %	16%	24%	32%	35%	37%	39%	39%	39%

High Volatility

STOCK PRICE — NUMBER OF MONTHS BEFORE THE OPTIONS EXPIRE

STOCK PRICE	1	2	3	4	5	6	7	8	9
35	0.0	0.0	0.0	0.1	0.3	0.4	0.5	0.8	1.0
35	1 %	2 %	9 %	13%	17%	19%	24%	26%	29%
34	0.0	0.0	0.1	0.3	0.4	0.6	0.8	1.0	1.3
34	1 %	6 %	12%	17%	20%	24%	28%	29%	32%
33	0.0	0.0	0.1	0.4	0.6	0.7	1.0	1.3	1.6
33	0 %	9 %	16%	20%	26%	30%	32%	36%	35%
32	0.0	0.1	0.3	0.6	0.8	1.0	1.4	1.7	2.0
32	2 %	13%	19%	27%	31%	32%	35%	36%	34%
31	0.0	0.2	0.4	0.8	1.1	1.3	1.6	2.1	2.4
31	6 %	20%	29%	33%	35%	35%	35%	35%	32%
30	0.0	0.4	0.7	1.2	1.5	1.8	2.1	2.4	2.8
30	12%	26%	34%	36%	36%	36%	36%	35%	33%
29	0.0	0.5	0.9	1.5	1.9	2.2	2.5	2.8	3.3
29	19%	35%	37%	37%	34%	33%	33%	35%	35%
28	0.2	0.9	1.4	1.9	2.3	2.6	3.0	3.4	3.8
28	36%	35%	36%	34%	37%	36%	36%	36%	36%
27	0.6	1.3	1.9	2.4	2.8	3.1	3.4	3.8	4.2
27	36%	35%	37%	37%	38%	40%	37%	36%	38%
26	1.0	1.8	2.3	2.9	3.3	3.6	3.8	4.3	4.7
26	35%	37%	41%	36%	36%	39%	39%	40%	40%
25	1.5	2.3	2.8	3.4	3.9	4.1	4.4	4.8	5.2
25	42%	41%	42%	42%	42%	42%	42%	40%	36%
24	2.3	3.1	3.6	4.1	4.5	4.8	5.1	5.4	5.8
24	35%	37%	41%	36%	36%	39%	39%	40%	40%
23	3.2	4.0	4.5	5.0	5.3	5.5	5.9	6.2	6.6
23	36%	35%	37%	37%	38%	40%	37%	36%	38%
22	4.1	4.8	5.3	5.8	6.2	6.4	6.6	7.0	7.4
22	36%	35%	36%	34%	37%	36%	36%	36%	36%
21	5.1	5.7	6.2	6.7	7.0	7.2	7.4	7.8	8.2
21	19%	35%	37%	37%	34%	33%	33%	35%	35%
20	6.0	6.7	7.1	7.5	7.9	8.1	8.3	8.4	8.4
20	12%	26%	34%	36%	36%	36%	36%	35%	33%

HIGH PRICE PUT TABLE

Exercise Price is (30)

Average Volatility

STOCK PRICE — NUMBER OF MONTHS BEFORE THE OPTIONS EXPIRE

STOCK PRICE	1	2	3	4	5	6	7	8	9
40	0.0	0.0	0.0	0.0	0.0	0.1	0.1	0.2	0.3
40	1 %	1 %	4 %	7 %	10%	18%	19%	25%	25%
39	0.0	0.0	0.0	0.0	0.1	0.2	0.2	0.4	0.5
39	1 %	1 %	4 %	10%	20%	23%	25%	26%	31%
38	0.0	0.0	0.0	0.1	0.2	0.3	0.4	0.5	0.7
38	1 %	4 %	9 %	20%	25%	26%	30%	34%	35%
37	0.0	0.0	0.0	0.2	0.3	0.4	0.6	0.8	1.0
37	1 %	7 %	19%	24%	30%	34%	35%	37%	38%
36	0.0	0.0	0.1	0.3	0.5	0.6	0.8	1.0	1.3
36	1 %	17%	24%	32%	37%	39%	39%	39%	40%
35	0.0	0.0	0.2	0.5	0.7	0.9	1.1	1.4	1.6
35	5 %	24%	33%	36%	40%	39%	39%	40%	39%
34	0.0	0.1	0.4	0.8	1.0	1.3	1.5	1.8	2.0
34	18%	34%	39%	39%	39%	40%	39%	39%	39%
33	0.0	0.4	0.8	1.2	1.4	1.7	1.9	2.2	2.5
33	33%	40%	39%	39%	38%	38%	39%	38%	38%
32	0.3	0.8	1.1	1.6	1.9	2.1	2.3	2.7	2.9
32	39%	39%	39%	36%	37%	36%	36%	34%	35%
31	0.7	1.2	1.6	2.1	2.3	2.6	2.8	3.0	3.4
31	40%	40%	37%	36%	36%	35%	39%	39%	38%
30	1.1	1.7	2.1	2.5	2.8	3.1	3.3	3.5	3.9
30	37%	38%	38%	40%	43%	41%	40%	42%	41%
29	1.9	2.5	2.8	3.3	3.6	3.8	4.0	4.3	4.6
29	40%	40%	37%	36%	36%	35%	39%	39%	38%
28	2.9	3.4	3.7	4.2	4.4	4.6	4.8	5.1	5.4
28	39%	39%	39%	36%	37%	36%	36%	34%	35%
27	3.8	4.3	4.6	4.9	5.2	5.4	5.6	5.9	6.2
27	33%	40%	39%	39%	38%	38%	39%	38%	38%
26	4.8	5.2	5.5	5.9	6.1	6.3	6.5	6.7	7.0
26	18%	34%	39%	39%	39%	40%	39%	39%	39%
25	5.7	6.2	6.4	6.8	7.0	7.2	7.4	7.6	7.9
25	5 %	24%	33%	36%	40%	39%	39%	40%	39%

High Volatility

STOCK PRICE — NUMBER OF MONTHS BEFORE THE OPTIONS EXPIRE

STOCK PRICE	1	2	3	4	5	6	7	8	9
40	0.0	0.0	0.2	0.4	0.7	1.0	1.2	1.5	1.9
40	1 %	8 %	14%	20%	26%	29%	30%	32%	33%
39	0.0	0.1	0.3	0.6	0.9	1.2	1.5	1.8	2.3
39	1 %	12%	20%	26%	30%	31%	34%	35%	35%
38	0.0	0.1	0.4	0.8	1.1	1.5	1.8	2.2	2.6
38	2 %	16%	25%	31%	33%	35%	35%	35%	34%
37	0.0	0.3	0.6	1.1	1.5	1.8	2.2	2.6	3.1
37	7 %	20%	30%	31%	33%	35%	35%	36%	32%
36	0.0	0.4	0.9	1.4	1.9	2.2	2.6	3.0	3.5
36	12%	29%	34%	36%	34%	36%	35%	32%	32%
35	0.0	0.6	1.1	1.8	2.2	2.6	2.9	3.4	3.9
35	20%	33%	35%	34%	32%	32%	33%	35%	36%
34	0.2	0.9	1.6	2.3	2.7	3.0	3.4	3.9	4.4
34	30%	36%	36%	34%	35%	36%	36%	37%	38%
33	0.5	1.4	2.0	2.7	3.2	3.5	3.9	4.3	4.9
33	36%	36%	33%	36%	35%	37%	39%	36%	37%
32	0.9	1.8	2.5	3.1	3.7	4.0	4.3	4.8	5.3
32	37%	34%	37%	40%	37%	35%	38%	39%	40%
31	1.4	2.3	2.9	3.6	4.2	4.5	4.9	5.3	5.8
31	34%	38%	40%	37%	38%	41%	40%	40%	41%
30	1.8	2.8	3.5	4.2	4.6	5.0	5.3	5.8	6.3
30	42%	40%	41%	42%	42%	42%	42%	38%	37%
29	2.7	3.6	4.2	4.9	5.4	5.7	6.0	6.5	7.0
29	34%	38%	40%	37%	38%	41%	40%	40%	41%
28	3.6	4.5	5.0	5.7	6.2	6.5	6.8	7.3	7.7
28	37%	34%	37%	40%	37%	35%	38%	39%	40%
27	4.5	5.3	5.9	6.5	6.9	7.2	7.5	8.0	8.3
27	36%	36%	33%	36%	35%	37%	39%	36%	37%
26	5.4	6.2	6.7	7.3	7.8	8.1	8.4	8.4	9.1
26	30%	36%	36%	34%	35%	36%	36%	37%	38%
25	6.4	7.1	7.6	8.2	8.5	8.5	9.2	9.2	9.9
25	20%	33%	35%	34%	32%	32%	33%	35%	36%

HIGH PRICE PUT TABLE
Exercise Price is (35)

Average Volatility

STOCK PRICE — NUMBER OF MONTHS BEFORE THE OPTIONS EXPIRE

STOCK PRICE	1	2	3	4	5	6	7	8	9
45	0.0	0.0	0.0	0.1	0.1	0.2	0.4	0.5	0.7
45	1 %	4 %	7 %	16%	21%	25%	26%	31%	32%
44	0.0	0.0	0.0	0.1	0.3	0.4	0.5	0.7	0.9
44	1 %	4 %	11%	21%	25%	27%	32%	34%	35%
43	0.0	0.0	0.1	0.2	0.4	0.6	0.7	1.0	1.2
43	1 %	9 %	19%	24%	32%	34%	36%	38%	39%
42	0.0	0.0	0.2	0.4	0.6	0.8	1.0	1.3	1.6
42	2 %	17%	24%	32%	35%	38%	39%	39%	39%
41	0.0	0.0	0.2	0.5	0.8	1.0	1.2	1.5	1.9
41	4 %	25%	33%	38%	39%	39%	39%	39%	39%
40	0.0	0.1	0.5	0.8	1.1	1.4	1.7	2.0	2.3
40	12%	32%	38%	39%	40%	39%	39%	39%	38%
39	0.0	0.4	0.8	1.2	1.5	1.8	2.0	2.3	2.7
39	25%	38%	39%	40%	39%	39%	39%	39%	38%
38	0.1	0.7	1.1	1.6	2.0	2.2	2.4	2.8	3.2
38	38%	40%	39%	38%	37%	38%	39%	37%	35%
37	0.5	1.1	1.6	2.0	2.4	2.6	2.9	3.3	3.6
37	39%	38%	38%	36%	36%	35%	35%	35%	35%
36	0.8	1.5	2.0	2.5	2.8	3.1	3.4	3.7	4.1
36	39%	36%	36%	35%	37%	38%	40%	40%	39%
35	1.3	2.0	2.5	3.0	3.4	3.6	3.9	4.2	4.6
35	37%	39%	38%	40%	43%	41%	40%	43%	43%
34	2.1	2.8	3.3	3.8	4.1	4.3	4.6	5.0	5.3
34	39%	36%	36%	35%	37%	38%	40%	40%	39%
33	3.1	3.7	4.1	4.6	4.9	5.2	5.5	5.8	6.1
33	39%	38%	38%	36%	36%	35%	35%	35%	35%
32	4.0	4.6	5.0	5.4	5.7	6.0	6.2	6.5	6.8
32	38%	40%	39%	38%	37%	38%	39%	37%	35%
31	4.9	5.5	5.9	6.3	6.6	6.8	7.0	7.3	7.6
31	25%	38%	39%	40%	39%	39%	39%	39%	38%
30	5.9	6.5	6.8	7.2	7.5	7.7	7.9	8.2	8.5
30	12%	32%	38%	39%	40%	39%	39%	39%	38%

High Volatility

STOCK PRICE — NUMBER OF MONTHS BEFORE THE OPTIONS EXPIRE

STOCK PRICE	1	2	3	4	5	6	7	8	9
45	0.0	0.1	0.4	0.9	1.3	1.6	1.9	2.4	2.9
45	4 %	20%	24%	31%	32%	32%	32%	32%	32%
44	0.0	0.2	0.6	1.1	1.6	1.9	2.2	2.7	3.3
44	3 %	23%	26%	32%	32%	33%	34%	33%	32%
43	0.0	0.4	0.8	1.4	1.8	2.2	2.7	3.2	3.7
43	9 %	25%	32%	32%	32%	34%	33%	32%	33%
42	0.0	0.6	1.1	1.8	2.3	2.6	3.0	3.6	4.1
42	15%	31%	32%	32%	32%	32%	34%	35%	34%
41	0.0	0.7	1.3	2.1	2.6	3.0	3.5	4.0	4.6
41	23%	33%	32%	32%	33%	34%	34%	35%	35%
40	0.2	1.0	1.7	2.6	3.1	3.4	3.9	4.4	5.1
40	30%	32%	32%	34%	35%	35%	36%	35%	35%
39	0.4	1.4	2.1	3.0	3.5	3.9	4.4	5.0	5.5
39	33%	32%	35%	36%	35%	37%	35%	35%	36%
38	0.8	1.9	2.6	3.5	4.0	4.4	4.8	5.4	6.0
38	33%	36%	34%	37%	35%	36%	36%	37%	38%
37	1.2	2.3	3.1	3.9	4.5	4.9	5.3	5.9	6.4
37	35%	37%	37%	37%	38%	37%	38%	38%	39%
36	1.7	2.8	3.6	4.4	5.0	5.4	5.8	6.4	6.9
36	36%	39%	39%	40%	39%	40%	39%	40%	37%
35	2.2	3.4	4.1	5.0	5.5	5.9	6.3	6.8	7.4
35	40%	40%	40%	41%	40%	40%	39%	39%	39%
34	3.0	4.1	4.8	5.7	6.2	6.6	7.0	7.6	8.1
34	36%	39%	39%	40%	39%	40%	39%	40%	37%
33	3.9	5.0	5.6	6.5	7.0	7.3	7.7	8.3	8.4
33	35%	37%	37%	37%	38%	37%	38%	38%	39%
32	4.8	5.8	6.5	7.3	7.8	8.2	8.4	8.4	9.2
32	33%	36%	34%	37%	35%	36%	36%	37%	38%
31	5.8	6.7	7.3	8.1	8.5	8.5	9.2	9.2	10.
31	33%	32%	35%	36%	35%	37%	35%	35%	36%
30	6.7	7.6	8.2	8.6	9.3	9.3	10.	10.	10.
30	30%	32%	32%	34%	35%	35%	36%	35%	35%

HIGH PRICE PUT TABLE

Exercise Price is (40)

Average Volatility

STOCK PRICE — NUMBER OF MONTHS BEFORE THE OPTIONS EXPIRE

STOCK PRICE	1	2	3	4	5	6	7	8	9
50	0.0	0.0	0.0	0.2	0.3	0.5	0.7	0.9	1.2
50	1 $	4 $	13$	22$	26$	30$	33$	35$	36$
49	0.0	0.0	0.1	0.3	0.5	0.7	0.9	1.2	1.5
49	1 $	9 $	19$	25$	31$	34$	35$	38$	38$
48	0.0	0.0	0.2	0.4	0.7	0.9	1.2	1.5	1.8
48	1 $	18$	24$	32$	35$	38$	40$	40$	39$
47	0.0	0.0	0.2	0.6	0.9	1.2	1.4	1.8	2.1
47	4 $	22$	32$	36$	38$	40$	39$	39$	39$
46	0.0	0.1	0.4	0.9	1.2	1.5	1.8	2.2	2.6
46	10$	31$	38$	39$	39$	39$	40$	40$	38$
45	0.0	0.3	0.8	1.2	1.7	2.0	2.2	2.5	2.9
45	21$	37$	39$	39$	38$	39$	39$	39$	38$
44	0.1	0.6	1.1	1.6	2.0	2.3	2.6	2.9	3.4
44	33$	39$	39$	39$	38$	38$	39$	38$	36$
43	0.3	1.0	1.5	2.1	2.4	2.8	3.1	3.4	3.9
43	39$	39$	39$	37$	37$	37$	36$	36$	35$
42	0.7	1.4	1.9	2.4	2.9	3.3	3.5	3.9	4.3
42	39$	39$	37$	36$	35$	35$	35$	36$	36$
41	1.1	1.9	2.4	2.9	3.3	3.7	4.0	4.3	4.7
41	40$	36$	36$	37$	39$	38$	40$	39$	38$
40	1.6	2.3	2.8	3.4	3.9	4.2	4.5	4.8	5.3
40	37$	38$	39$	42$	42$	41$	41$	44$	43$
39	2.4	3.1	3.6	4.2	4.6	4.9	5.2	5.6	6.1
39	40$	36$	36$	37$	39$	38$	40$	39$	38$
38	3.2	4.0	4.5	5.0	5.4	5.7	6.1	6.4	6.8
38	39$	39$	37$	36$	35$	35$	35$	36$	36$
37	4.2	4.9	5.4	5.9	6.3	6.5	6.8	7.1	7.6
37	39$	39$	39$	37$	37$	37$	36$	36$	35$
36	5.1	5.8	6.2	6.7	7.0	7.3	7.5	7.9	8.2
36	33$	39$	39$	39$	38$	38$	39$	38$	36$
35	6.1	6.7	7.1	7.6	7.9	8.2	8.4	8.7	8.7
35	21$	37$	39$	39$	38$	39$	39$	39$	38$

High Volatility

STOCK PRICE — NUMBER OF MONTHS BEFORE THE OPTIONS EXPIRE

STOCK PRICE	1	2	3	4	5	6	7	8	9
50	0.0	0.3	0.8	1.4	1.9	2.3	2.7	3.2	4.1
50	7 $	23$	30$	32$	32$	32$	33$	32$	33$
49	0.0	0.5	1.0	1.7	2.2	2.7	3.1	3.7	4.4
49	11$	25$	32$	33$	33$	33$	32$	34$	34$
48	0.1	0.6	1.3	2.0	2.6	3.1	3.6	4.1	4.8
48	16$	33$	33$	33$	32$	32$	33$	34$	34$
47	0.1	0.8	1.6	2.4	3.0	3.5	4.0	4.5	5.3
47	23$	32$	32$	32$	34$	34$	34$	35$	35$
46	0.2	1.1	1.9	2.9	3.5	4.0	4.4	5.0	5.8
46	27$	32$	33$	35$	35$	35$	35$	36$	35$
45	0.4	1.5	2.3	3.3	3.9	4.3	4.9	5.5	6.3
45	32$	34$	34$	36$	35$	35$	35$	35$	35$
44	0.7	1.9	2.8	3.7	4.3	4.9	5.4	5.9	6.8
44	34$	35$	36$	35$	36$	35$	34$	36$	37$
43	1.0	2.4	3.2	4.2	4.9	5.3	5.9	6.4	7.3
43	34$	35$	36$	37$	37$	37$	37$	39$	38$
42	1.6	2.8	3.8	4.7	5.3	5.8	6.3	6.9	7.6
42	35$	37$	38$	37$	37$	37$	38$	38$	38$
41	2.0	3.3	4.2	5.2	5.8	6.3	6.8	7.4	8.2
41	38$	40$	38$	40$	40$	40$	39$	39$	38$
40	2.6	3.9	4.8	5.7	6.3	6.8	7.3	7.9	8.5
40	40$	40$	40$	40$	40$	40$	39$	39$	39$
39	3.4	4.7	5.5	6.4	7.0	7.5	8.0	8.4	9.2
39	38$	40$	38$	40$	40$	40$	39$	39$	38$
38	4.2	5.5	6.3	7.2	7.8	8.2	8.4	9.2	10.
38	35$	37$	38$	37$	37$	37$	38$	38$	38$
37	5.2	6.3	7.2	8.1	8.5	8.5	9.2	10.	10.
37	34$	35$	36$	37$	37$	37$	37$	39$	38$
36	6.1	7.2	8.0	8.5	9.3	9.3	10.	10.	10.
36	34$	35$	36$	35$	36$	35$	34$	36$	37$
35	7.0	8.1	8.7	9.4	10.	10.	10.	10.	11.
35	32$	32$	34$	36$	35$	35$	35$	35$	35$

163

HIGH PRICE PUT TABLE

Exercise Price is ⟨45⟩

Average Volatility

STOCK PRICE — NUMBER OF MONTHS BEFORE THE OPTIONS EXPIRE

STOCK PRICE	1	2	3	4	5	6	7	8	9
55	0.0	0.0	0.2	0.4	0.7	0.9	1.1	1.3	1.8
55	1%	10%	20%	27%	30%	34%	35%	39%	39%
54	0.0	0.1	0.3	0.6	0.9	1.1	1.4	1.7	2.1
54	2%	17%	24%	31%	32%	37%	38%	40%	38%
53	0.0	0.1	0.4	0.7	1.2	1.4	1.8	2.0	2.5
53	4%	22%	31%	36%	36%	39%	39%	39%	39%
52	0.0	0.2	0.5	1.0	1.4	1.7	2.1	2.4	2.9
52	9%	26%	34%	39%	37%	39%	38%	39%	38%
51	0.0	0.3	0.8	1.3	1.8	2.1	2.5	2.7	3.2
51	20%	34%	39%	39%	37%	39%	39%	39%	37%
50	0.1	0.6	1.1	1.7	2.2	2.5	2.9	3.2	3.6
50	25%	38%	39%	39%	36%	38%	38%	38%	36%
49	0.2	0.9	1.4	2.0	2.6	2.8	3.3	3.6	4.1
49	35%	39%	39%	39%	36%	37%	35%	39%	34%
48	0.6	1.3	1.9	2.5	3.0	3.3	3.8	4.0	4.6
48	39%	38%	38%	37%	34%	34%	35%	36%	34%
47	0.9	1.7	2.3	2.9	3.6	3.9	4.2	4.5	5.0
47	38%	36%	36%	36%	35%	36%	34%	39%	36%
46	1.3	2.2	2.7	3.4	4.0	4.2	4.6	4.9	5.5
46	36%	36%	36%	37%	36%	39%	40%	40%	38%
45	1.8	2.7	3.3	3.9	4.5	4.8	5.1	5.5	6.0
45	36%	38%	38%	41%	37%	41%	40%	43%	43%
44	2.6	3.4	4.0	4.6	5.2	5.5	5.9	6.2	6.8
44	36%	36%	36%	37%	36%	39%	40%	40%	38%
43	3.5	4.3	4.9	5.4	6.1	6.3	6.7	6.9	7.5
43	38%	36%	36%	36%	35%	36%	34%	39%	36%
42	4.5	5.3	5.7	6.3	6.9	7.2	7.5	7.7	8.3
42	39%	38%	38%	37%	34%	34%	35%	36%	34%
41	5.4	6.1	6.6	7.1	7.7	7.9	8.2	8.5	8.6
41	35%	39%	39%	39%	36%	37%	35%	39%	34%
40	6.3	7.0	7.4	8.0	8.6	8.7	8.7	8.7	9.5
40	25%	38%	39%	39%	36%	38%	38%	38%	36%

High Volatility

STOCK PRICE — NUMBER OF MONTHS BEFORE THE OPTIONS EXPIRE

STOCK PRICE	1	2	3	4	5	6	7	8	9
55	0.1	0.6	1.2	1.9	2.9	3.2	3.8	4.2	5.2
55	12%	26%	32%	33%	32%	32%	32%	33%	34%
54	0.1	0.8	1.5	2.3	3.2	3.5	4.2	4.6	5.6
54	14%	31%	32%	32%	32%	33%	33%	34%	34%
53	0.2	1.0	1.8	2.7	3.7	4.0	4.7	5.1	6.2
53	23%	32%	32%	32%	33%	34%	34%	35%	35%
52	0.3	1.3	2.1	3.1	4.1	4.4	5.1	5.5	6.6
52	25%	32%	32%	35%	32%	35%	35%	35%	35%
51	0.5	1.6	2.6	3.6	4.6	4.9	5.5	6.0	7.0
51	32%	32%	34%	35%	34%	35%	34%	35%	35%
50	0.8	2.0	3.0	4.0	5.1	5.3	6.0	6.5	7.4
50	33%	32%	35%	35%	35%	36%	35%	36%	36%
49	1.1	2.4	3.5	4.5	5.5	5.9	6.5	6.9	8.0
49	32%	35%	34%	37%	35%	35%	33%	38%	38%
48	1.5	2.9	3.8	4.9	6.0	6.3	7.0	7.4	8.5
48	33%	34%	37%	37%	34%	37%	38%	39%	37%
47	2.0	3.4	4.4	5.5	6.5	6.8	7.4	7.9	8.8
47	31%	37%	38%	37%	37%	38%	38%	40%	38%
46	2.5	3.9	4.9	5.9	7.0	7.2	7.9	8.4	8.6
46	35%	40%	39%	40%	37%	41%	38%	37%	36%
45	3.0	4.5	5.4	6.5	7.5	7.8	8.5	8.5	9.3
45	40%	40%	40%	40%	39%	38%	38%	39%	38%
44	3.8	5.2	6.1	7.2	8.2	8.4	8.4	9.3	10.
44	35%	40%	39%	40%	37%	41%	38%	37%	36%
43	4.7	6.0	6.9	8.0	8.4	9.3	9.3	10.	10.
43	31%	37%	38%	37%	37%	38%	38%	40%	38%
42	5.6	6.9	7.7	8.5	9.3	9.3	10.	10.	11.
42	33%	34%	37%	37%	34%	37%	38%	39%	37%
41	6.5	7.7	8.5	9.4	10.	10.	10.	11.	12.
41	32%	35%	34%	37%	35%	35%	33%	38%	38%
40	7.4	8.7	8.7	10.	11.	11.	11.	12.	13.
40	33%	32%	35%	35%	35%	36%	35%	36%	36%

HIGH PRICE PUT TABLE
Exercise Price is (50)

Average Volatility

NUMBER OF MONTHS BEFORE THE OPTIONS EXPIRE

Stock Price	1	2	3	4	5	6	7	8	9
65	0.0	0.0	0.0	0.1	0.2	0.3	0.5	0.7	0.9
65	1%	1%	4%	11%	17%	21%	24%	25%	28%
64	0.0	0.0	0.0	0.1	0.2	0.4	0.5	0.7	1.0
64	1%	4%	6%	18%	21%	25%	26%	31%	34%
63	0.0	0.0	0.0	0.2	0.4	0.5	0.7	1.0	1.3
63	1%	4%	9%	20%	25%	26%	31%	35%	34%
62	0.0	0.0	0.0	0.2	0.4	0.7	0.9	1.2	1.5
62	1%	5%	17%	25%	27%	32%	35%	37%	39%
61	0.0	0.0	0.1	0.4	0.6	0.9	1.1	1.5	1.8
61	1%	9%	19%	26%	32%	35%	37%	39%	39%
60	0.0	0.1	0.2	0.5	0.8	1.1	1.3	1.6	2.0
60	1%	14%	25%	32%	35%	39%	39%	39%	39%
59	0.0	0.1	0.4	0.8	1.1	1.4	1.8	2.2	2.6
59	3%	21%	29%	35%	38%	39%	39%	39%	40%
58	0.0	0.1	0.4	0.8	1.2	1.5	1.8	2.2	2.6
58	6%	24%	35%	39%	39%	41%	41%	41%	39%
57	0.0	0.3	0.8	1.3	1.7	2.1	2.5	2.9	3.3
57	13%	30%	37%	38%	39%	39%	39%	39%	38%
56	0.0	0.5	0.9	1.5	1.9	2.2	2.6	3.0	3.5
56	22%	38%	39%	40%	39%	40%	40%	39%	39%
55	0.1	0.8	1.4	2.0	2.5	2.8	3.2	3.7	4.3
55	29%	39%	39%	40%	38%	39%	39%	38%	35%
54	0.3	1.1	1.6	2.2	2.7	3.1	3.4	3.9	4.4
54	39%	39%	41%	39%	39%	40%	40%	41%	37%
53	0.7	1.6	2.2	2.8	3.4	3.8	4.2	4.6	5.2
53	39%	38%	38%	35%	35%	34%	34%	34%	33%
52	0.9	1.8	2.5	3.1	3.7	4.0	4.4	4.8	5.3
52	40%	39%	40%	38%	37%	37%	38%	39%	39%
51	1.4	2.4	3.1	3.8	4.3	4.7	5.1	5.5	5.9
51	39%	36%	36%	35%	38%	39%	40%	39%	38%
50	1.9	2.8	3.4	4.1	4.5	5.0	5.3	5.7	6.3
50	37%	38%	39%	44%	43%	42%	41%	43%	43%
49	2.6	3.6	4.2	4.9	5.4	5.9	6.2	6.7	7.2
49	39%	36%	36%	35%	38%	39%	40%	39%	38%
48	3.5	4.4	5.0	5.6	6.0	6.4	6.8	7.3	7.8
48	40%	39%	40%	38%	37%	37%	38%	39%	39%
47	4.5	5.3	5.9	6.5	7.0	7.4	7.8	8.1	8.5
47	39%	38%	38%	35%	35%	34%	34%	34%	33%
46	5.4	6.2	6.8	7.3	7.8	8.1	8.5	8.6	8.6
46	39%	39%	41%	39%	39%	40%	40%	41%	37%
45	6.3	7.1	7.6	8.2	8.6	8.8	8.8	9.5	9.5
45	29%	39%	39%	40%	38%	39%	39%	38%	35%

High Volatility

NUMBER OF MONTHS BEFORE THE OPTIONS EXPIRE

Stock Price	1	2	3	4	5	6	7	8	9
65	0.0	0.2	0.5	1.2	1.6	2.0	2.5	3.0	3.7
65	3%	14%	23%	25%	31%	32%	32%	32%	33%
64	0.0	0.2	0.6	1.3	1.7	2.1	2.6	3.1	3.8
64	4%	19%	24%	30%	32%	33%	33%	33%	34%
63	0.0	0.3	0.8	1.6	2.1	2.5	3.1	3.8	4.4
63	4%	22%	27%	32%	32%	33%	33%	34%	32%
62	0.0	0.4	1.0	1.7	2.4	2.8	3.3	4.0	4.7
62	8%	24%	32%	32%	32%	32%	34%	34%	35%
61	0.0	0.6	1.2	2.0	2.7	3.3	3.8	4.6	5.3
61	10%	25%	32%	32%	32%	33%	33%	33%	33%
60	0.1	0.7	1.4	2.3	2.9	3.4	3.9	4.7	5.5
60	14%	31%	33%	34%	34%	34%	34%	35%	35%
59	0.2	1.0	1.8	2.8	3.5	4.0	4.7	5.4	6.1
59	21%	32%	34%	32%	32%	33%	33%	34%	35%
58	0.2	1.1	1.9	3.0	3.7	4.3	4.9	5.6	6.4
58	26%	34%	35%	35%	35%	37%	36%	35%	35%
57	0.4	1.6	2.5	3.5	4.4	4.9	5.5	6.2	7.1
57	29%	32%	34%	34%	35%	35%	35%	35%	36%
56	0.5	1.8	2.7	3.9	4.5	5.1	5.7	6.5	7.2
56	33%	34%	35%	35%	35%	37%	36%	36%	36%
55	0.9	2.3	3.3	4.4	5.3	5.8	6.5	7.2	8.0
55	33%	34%	35%	35%	36%	35%	35%	35%	38%
54	1.1	2.6	3.6	4.7	5.5	6.1	6.7	7.5	8.1
54	36%	36%	35%	37%	38%	38%	38%	39%	40%
53	1.7	3.3	4.3	5.4	6.3	6.9	7.4	8.1	9.0
53	35%	34%	37%	37%	36%	37%	38%	38%	40%
52	2.0	3.7	4.6	5.8	6.6	7.1	7.6	8.4	8.8
52	35%	37%	40%	38%	38%	40%	39%	40%	40%
51	2.6	4.2	5.2	6.4	7.1	7.7	8.3	8.6	9.5
51	37%	40%	39%	40%	40%	40%	40%	40%	37%
50	3.0	4.6	5.6	6.8	7.5	8.1	8.5	9.3	10.
50	41%	41%	41%	40%	40%	40%	40%	40%	40%
49	3.8	5.4	6.4	7.6	8.4	8.4	9.3	10.	10.
49	37%	40%	39%	40%	40%	40%	40%	40%	37%
48	4.6	6.11	7.1	8.2	8.5	9.3	9.3	10.	10.
48	35%	37%	40%	38%	38%	40%	39%	40%	40%
47	5.6	7.0	8.0	8.5	9.3	10.	10.	10.	11.
47	35%	34%	37%	37%	36%	37%	38%	38%	40%
46	6.5	7.9	8.6	9.4	10.	11.	11.	11.	12.
46	36%	36%	35%	37%	38%	38%	38%	39%	40%
45	7.4	8.8	9.5	10.	11.	11.	11.	12.	13.
45	33%	34%	35%	35%	36%	35%	35%	35%	38%

HIGH PRICE PUT TABLE

Exercise Price is (60)

Average Volatility

STOCK PRICE — NUMBER OF MONTHS BEFORE THE OPTIONS EXPIRE

Stock Price	1	2	3	4	5	6	7	8	9
75	0.0	0.0	0.1	0.4	0.6	0.8	1.1	1.4	1.9
75	1%	4%	12%	21%	24%	28%	32%	34%	36%
74	0.0	0.0	0.1	0.4	0.7	0.9	1.1	1.5	1.8
74	1%	6%	19%	25%	29%	34%	37%	39%	39%
73	0.0	0.0	0.2	0.6	0.9	1.2	1.5	1.9	2.4
73	0%	9%	21%	26%	32%	34%	37%	39%	39%
72	0.0	0.0	0.3	0.7	1.1	1.4	1.7	2.1	2.5
72	1%	17%	24%	32%	35%	38%	39%	39%	39%
71	0.0	0.1	0.4	0.9	1.3	1.7	2.1	2.6	3.1
71	4%	19%	27%	35%	38%	39%	39%	39%	39%
70	0.0	0.1	0.5	1.0	1.4	1.8	2.2	2.7	3.2
70	5%	25%	35%	38%	40%	39%	39%	40%	39%
69	0.0	0.3	0.8	1.4	1.9	2.4	2.8	3.3	3.9
69	9%	28%	35%	39%	39%	39%	39%	39%	39%
68	0.0	0.4	0.9	1.5	2.1	2.5	2.8	3.4	3.9
68	18%	35%	39%	40%	40%	39%	41%	39%	39%
67	0.1	0.8	1.4	2.0	2.7	3.2	3.6	4.1	4.6
67	25%	36%	39%	39%	38%	39%	39%	38%	36%
66	0.2	0.9	1.5	2.3	2.8	3.3	3.7	4.3	4.8
66	31%	39%	41%	39%	39%	39%	39%	39%	40%
65	0.4	1.3	2.1	2.9	3.4	3.9	4.5	5.0	5.7
65	37%	39%	39%	37%	37%	36%	36%	37%	34%
64	0.7	1.6	2.3	3.0	3.7	4.1	4.6	5.1	5.8
64	39%	40%	39%	39%	39%	39%	40%	38%	37%
63	1.0	2.1	2.9	3.8	4.4	4.9	5.4	5.9	6.5
63	39%	36%	35%	34%	35%	35%	35%	33%	35%
62	1.4	2.4	3.2	4.1	4.6	5.1	5.5	6.1	6.6
62	39%	40%	38%	37%	38%	39%	39%	40%	39%
61	1.9	3.1	3.8	4.7	5.3	5.8	6.3	6.8	7.3
61	38%	35%	36%	37%	38%	39%	39%	40%	39%
60	2.3	3.4	4.2	5.1	5.6	6.1	6.5	7.0	7.7
60	37%	38%	39%	42%	43%	41%	42%	42%	43%
59	3.0	4.2	5.0	5.8	6.4	7.0	7.4	8.0	8.5
59	38%	35%	36%	37%	38%	39%	39%	40%	39%
58	3.8	4.9	5.6	6.5	7.0	7.5	7.9	8.5	8.5
58	39%	40%	38%	37%	38%	39%	39%	40%	39%
57	4.9	5.9	6.7	7.5	8.0	8.6	8.6	9.4	9.4
57	39%	36%	35%	34%	35%	35%	35%	33%	35%
56	5.8	6.8	7.4	8.2	8.7	8.7	9.5	9.5	10.
56	39%	40%	39%	39%	39%	39%	40%	38%	37%
55	6.7	7.8	8.5	8.8	9.6	9.6	10.	10.	11.
55	37%	39%	39%	37%	37%	36%	36%	37%	34%

High Volatility

STOCK PRICE — NUMBER OF MONTHS BEFORE THE OPTIONS EXPIRE

Stock Price	1	2	3	4	5	6	7	8	9
75	0.0	0.6	1.2	2.2	2.8	3.5	4.0	4.8	5.8
75	6%	23%	27%	32%	32%	32%	33%	32%	32%
74	0.0	0.7	1.3	2.3	3.0	3.5	4.0	4.9	5.9
74	10%	25%	32%	32%	33%	35%	34%	34%	34%
73	0.1	0.8	1.6	2.6	3.5	4.2	4.8	5.7	6.8
73	12%	26%	33%	33%	32%	32%	33%	34%	33%
72	0.1	1.0	1.9	2.9	3.7	4.3	4.9	5.9	6.8
72	16%	30%	32%	32%	33%	33%	34%	34%	34%
71	0.2	1.2	2.2	3.4	4.2	5.0	5.7	6.6	7.6
71	21%	32%	32%	32%	32%	33%	33%	33%	35%
70	0.2	1.3	2.3	3.5	4.4	5.1	5.8	6.7	7.8
70	24%	32%	34%	34%	35%	34%	36%	35%	35%
69	0.4	1.7	2.8	4.2	5.0	5.8	6.5	7.5	8.5
69	25%	33%	34%	34%	35%	35%	36%	36%	36%
68	0.5	2.0	3.1	4.5	5.3	6.0	6.7	7.7	8.6
68	32%	34%	34%	35%	35%	35%	35%	36%	35%
67	0.8	2.4	3.7	5.1	5.9	6.7	7.4	8.3	9.4
67	32%	32%	34%	35%	35%	35%	35%	34%	35%
66	1.0	2.7	3.9	5.3	6.2	7.0	7.5	8.5	9.3
66	34%	36%	35%	37%	36%	36%	36%	37%	38%
65	1.4	3.3	4.6	5.9	6.9	7.7	8.3	9.2	10.
65	33%	36%	35%	37%	36%	36%	37%	37%	38%
64	1.8	3.6	4.8	6.3	7.1	7.9	8.6	9.0	9.9
64	36%	35%	38%	38%	37%	37%	38%	40%	41%
63	2.3	4.3	5.6	7.0	8.0	8.7	8.9	9.8	10.
63	35%	37%	37%	36%	37%	37%	38%	38%	38%
62	2.7	4.6	5.9	7.3	8.2	8.7	8.7	10.	11.
62	37%	38%	37%	39%	40%	41%	41%	40%	37%
61	3.2	5.2	6.5	7.9	8.6	9.5	9.5	11.	12.
61	38%	40%	39%	40%	40%	41%	41%	38%	37%
60	3.8	5.6	7.0	8.4	8.5	9.3	10.	11.	11.
60	40%	40%	40%	41%	40%	40%	41%	40%	40%
59	4.5	6.5	7.7	8.5	9.3	10.	11.	11.	12.
59	38%	40%	39%	40%	40%	41%	41%	38%	37%
58	5.2	7.1	8.4	9.3	10.	11.	11.	12.	13.
58	37%	38%	37%	39%	40%	41%	41%	40%	37%
57	6.2	8.0	8.6	10.	11.	11.	12.	13.	14.
57	35%	37%	37%	36%	37%	37%	38%	38%	38%
56	7.1	8.7	9.5	11.	11.	11.	12.	14.	15.
56	36%	35%	38%	38%	37%	37%	38%	40%	41%
55	8.1	9.6	10.	12.	12.	12.	13.	15.	15.
55	33%	36%	36%	35%	37%	36%	37%	37%	38%

HIGH PRICE PUT TABLE
Exercise Price is (70)

Average Volatility

STOCK PRICE	1	2	3	4	5	6	7	8	9
85	0.0	0.1	0.4	0.8	1.1	1.5	1.9	2.4	2.9
85	1 %	11%	22%	27%	33%	34%	37%	38%	39%
84	0.0	0.1	0.4	0.8	1.2	1.6	1.9	2.4	3.0
84	1 %	17%	24%	32%	36%	39%	39%	39%	39%
83	0.0	0.2	0.6	1.1	1.6	2.0	2.5	3.1	3.6
83	3 %	19%	26%	33%	36%	38%	39%	39%	39%
82	0.0	0.1	0.6	1.2	1.7	2.1	2.5	3.1	3.7
82	4 %	25%	32%	36%	39%	39%	39%	39%	40%
81	0.0	0.3	0.8	1.5	2.1	2.6	3.1	3.7	4.4
81	9 %	25%	35%	39%	39%	39%	39%	39%	38%
80	0.0	0.4	1.0	1.6	2.2	2.8	3.3	3.8	4.3
80	13%	32%	39%	39%	39%	39%	39%	39%	40%
79	0.0	0.6	1.4	2.2	2.8	3.4	3.9	4.5	5.1
79	19%	35%	38%	39%	39%	39%	39%	38%	38%
78	0.1	0.8	1.5	2.3	2.9	3.5	3.9	4.6	5.3
78	25%	39%	40%	41%	40%	39%	39%	39%	40%
77	0.3	1.3	2.1	2.9	3.6	4.2	4.6	5.4	6.1
77	30%	38%	39%	38%	39%	38%	38%	37%	35%
76	0.4	1.4	2.3	3.1	3.7	4.3	4.8	5.5	6.1
76	38%	41%	39%	40%	39%	40%	40%	39%	37%
75	0.8	1.9	2.9	3.7	4.4	5.1	5.6	6.3	7.0
75	39%	39%	38%	36%	37%	36%	36%	34%	34%
74	0.9	2.1	3.0	3.9	4.6	5.2	5.7	6.3	7.0
74	41%	39%	39%	40%	38%	38%	38%	38%	40%
73	1.5	2.7	3.7	4.6	5.4	6.1	6.5	7.1	7.8
73	39%	36%	35%	35%	36%	34%	34%	36%	38%
72	1.7	3.0	4.0	4.9	5.6	6.2	6.7	7.3	8.0
72	39%	39%	36%	38%	40%	39%	40%	41%	40%
71	2.3	3.7	4.6	5.6	6.2	6.8	7.4	8.0	8.6
71	36%	35%	35%	38%	39%	40%	39%	38%	39%
70	2.7	4.0	5.0	5.9	6.6	7.1	7.6	8.3	8.5
70	37%	38%	40%	42%	43%	41%	42%	43%	43%
69	3.5	4.9	5.7	6.7	7.4	8.1	8.5	8.5	9.3
69	36%	35%	35%	38%	39%	40%	39%	38%	39%
68	4.3	5.5	6.4	7.3	8.0	8.6	8.6	9.4	10.
68	39%	39%	36%	38%	40%	39%	40%	41%	40%
67	5.2	6.4	7.3	8.3	8.6	9.5	9.5	10.	11.
67	39%	36%	35%	35%	36%	34%	34%	36%	38%
66	6.1	7.3	8.2	8.8	9.6	9.6	10.	11.	12.
66	41%	39%	39%	40%	38%	38%	38%	38%	40%
65	7.2	8.3	8.9	9.7	10.	11.	11.	12.	12.
65	39%	39%	38%	36%	37%	36%	36%	34%	34%

High Volatility

STOCK PRICE	1	2	3	4	5	6	7	8	9
85	0.1	1.1	2.0	3.3	4.2	4.9	5.7	6.9	8.1
85	12%	25%	32%	32%	32%	33%	33%	33%	33%
84	0.2	1.2	2.1	3.4	4.3	5.1	5.9	6.9	8.0
84	15%	30%	32%	34%	34%	34%	34%	35%	35%
83	0.2	1.4	2.6	4.0	5.0	5.8	6.7	7.8	9.1
83	22%	33%	32%	32%	32%	34%	34%	34%	34%
82	0.2	1.6	2.8	4.2	5.1	6.0	6.8	7.8	9.1
82	23%	32%	33%	33%	34%	34%	36%	35%	35%
81	0.4	1.9	3.2	4.8	5.9	6.7	7.5	8.6	9.8
81	25%	32%	32%	33%	34%	35%	35%	35%	35%
80	0.5	2.1	3.4	4.9	6.1	6.8	7.6	8.8	9.7
80	30%	34%	34%	35%	35%	35%	35%	36%	36%
79	0.8	2.5	4.0	5.6	6.7	7.5	8.4	9.5	10.
79	33%	33%	34%	35%	35%	36%	35%	35%	34%
78	0.9	2.9	4.3	5.8	7.0	7.7	8.6	9.4	10.
78	33%	35%	35%	35%	36%	36%	36%	36%	37%
77	1.4	3.4	4.9	6.5	7.6	8.5	9.3	10.	11.
77	33%	35%	35%	35%	36%	35%	34%	35%	37%
76	1.5	3.6	5.1	6.7	7.8	8.6	9.2	10.	11.
76	35%	35%	35%	37%	38%	37%	37%	38%	38%
75	2.0	4.3	5.9	7.5	8.6	9.1	10.	10.	12.
75	34%	35%	37%	37%	38%	37%	37%	38%	38%
74	2.4	4.6	6.2	7.7	8.8	8.9	9.8	10.	12.
74	36%	38%	39%	37%	37%	40%	39%	40%	40%
73	3.0	5.4	6.9	8.5	8.8	9.7	10.	12.	13.
73	34%	37%	38%	37%	37%	39%	39%	38%	38%
72	3.4	5.7	7.2	8.7	9.6	10.	11.	12.	13.
72	36%	40%	39%	40%	41%	40%	40%	40%	37%
71	3.9	6.3	7.8	9.4	10.	11.	12.	12.	13.
71	38%	39%	40%	40%	40%	40%	40%	37%	38%
70	4.5	6.8	8.2	9.3	10.	11.	11.	13.	14.
70	41%	40%	40%	40%	40%	41%	41%	41%	40%
69	5.1	7.5	8.5	10.	11.	11.	12.	14.	15.
69	38%	39%	40%	40%	40%	40%	40%	37%	38%
68	5.9	8.1	9.4	11.	11.	12.	13.	14.	16.
68	36%	40%	39%	40%	41%	40%	40%	40%	37%
67	6.9	8.6	10.	11.	12.	13.	14.	15.	16.
67	34%	37%	38%	37%	37%	39%	39%	38%	38%
66	7.7	9.6	11.	12.	13.	14.	15.	16.	17.
66	36%	38%	39%	37%	37%	40%	39%	40%	40%
65	8.7	10.	12.	13.	14.	15.	16.	16.	18.
65	34%	35%	37%	37%	38%	37%	37%	38%	38%

HIGH PRICE PUT TABLE

Exercise Price is ⑧⓪

Average Volatility

STOCK PRICE	*NUMBER OF MONTHS BEFORE THE OPTIONS EXPIRE*								
	1	2	3	4	5	6	7	8	9
95	0.0	0.3	0.7	1.3	1.9	2.4	2.9	3.5	4.2
95	4 %	20%	25%	32%	35%	38%	39%	39%	38%
94	0.0	0.2	0.7	1.3	1.8	2.3	2.8	3.4	4.1
94	4 %	22%	33%	36%	39%	39%	39%	39%	39%
93	0.0	0.3	0.9	1.7	2.3	2.9	3.5	4.1	4.9
93	6 %	25%	34%	36%	38%	39%	39%	39%	38%
92	0.0	0.4	1.1	1.8	2.5	3.1	3.6	4.2	4.9
92	10%	28%	36%	40%	39%	39%	39%	39%	40%
91	0.0	0.6	1.4	2.3	3.0	3.6	4.2	4.9	5.7
91	17%	32%	38%	38%	38%	39%	39%	39%	38%
90	0.1	0.8	1.6	2.4	3.1	3.8	4.3	4.8	5.6
90	21%	38%	39%	39%	39%	39%	39%	39%	39%
89	0.2	1.2	2.0	3.0	3.7	4.4	5.0	5.6	6.6
89	24%	38%	39%	38%	38%	38%	39%	38%	36%
88	0.3	1.3	2.1	3.1	3.9	4.5	5.0	5.7	6.7
88	32%	39%	40%	40%	39%	39%	39%	40%	37%
87	0.6	1.8	2.7	3.7	4.6	5.2	5.9	6.6	7.5
87	35%	38%	39%	38%	36%	36%	36%	36%	35%
86	0.7	2.0	2.9	3.9	4.7	5.4	6.0	6.7	7.5
86	39%	40%	39%	39%	39%	39%	39%	38%	36%
85	1.1	2.5	3.6	4.6	5.5	6.2	6.8	7.5	8.3
85	39%	38%	36%	36%	34%	34%	34%	35%	34%
84	1.3	2.7	3.7	4.8	5.6	6.3	6.8	7.4	8.3
84	41%	39%	39%	39%	39%	38%	38%	41%	39%
83	1.9	3.4	4.4	5.6	6.5	7.2	7.6	8.4	8.8
83	38%	36%	35%	36%	35%	35%	36%	38%	38%
82	2.1	3.7	4.7	5.8	6.7	7.3	7.8	8.5	8.7
82	42%	36%	36%	39%	38%	39%	40%	40%	38%
81	2.7	4.3	5.4	6.5	7.4	8.0	8.6	8.6	9.4
81	36%	35%	37%	38%	39%	39%	39%	38%	39%
80	3.1	4.7	5.7	6.8	7.6	8.3	8.5	9.3	10.
80	37%	39%	40%	42%	42%	41%	43%	44%	45%
79	3.9	5.5	6.5	7.7	8.5	8.5	9.3	10.	11.
79	36%	35%	37%	38%	39%	39%	39%	38%	39%
78	4.6	6.2	7.2	8.2	8.6	9.4	9.4	10.	11.
78	42%	36%	36%	39%	38%	39%	40%	40%	38%
77	5.6	7.0	8.0	8.7	9.5	10.	11.	11.	12.
77	38%	36%	35%	36%	35%	35%	36%	38%	38%
76	6.5	7.9	8.8	9.6	10.	11.	11.	12.	12.
76	41%	39%	39%	39%	39%	38%	38%	41%	39%
75	7.5	8.9	9.7	10.	11.	12.	12.	12.	13.
75	39%	38%	36%	36%	34%	34%	34%	35%	34%

High Volatility

STOCK PRICE	*NUMBER OF MONTHS BEFORE THE OPTIONS EXPIRE*								
	1	2	3	4	5	6	7	8	9
95	0.3	1.7	2.9	4.5	5.7	6.7	7.6	8.8	10.
95	21%	32%	33%	32%	33%	33%	34%	34%	35%
94	0.3	1.7	3.0	4.6	5.7	6.7	7.6	8.8	9.9
94	24%	33%	35%	35%	35%	36%	37%	35%	35%
93	0.4	2.1	3.6	5.4	6.7	7.7	8.5	9.8	10.
93	24%	32%	33%	33%	34%	34%	34%	35%	36%
92	0.6	2.4	3.9	5.5	6.8	7.7	8.6	9.7	10.
92	26%	32%	34%	35%	35%	35%	35%	35%	35%
91	0.7	2.8	4.4	6.2	7.5	8.5	9.4	10.	11.
91	32%	32%	32%	35%	35%	35%	35%	35%	34%
90	0.9	2.9	4.5	6.4	7.6	8.6	9.5	10.	11.
90	33%	35%	36%	35%	35%	37%	36%	37%	36%
89	1.2	3.4	5.2	7.0	8.4	9.4	10.	11.	12.
89	33%	32%	35%	36%	35%	35%	36%	34%	36%
88	1.4	3.8	5.5	7.3	8.6	9.3	10.	11.	13.
88	34%	35%	35%	37%	35%	36%	36%	37%	38%
87	1.9	4.3	6.1	8.0	9.2	10.	11.	12.	13.
87	33%	35%	34%	36%	36%	35%	37%	37%	38%
86	2.1	4.6	6.3	8.2	9.1	10.	10.	11.	13.
86	36%	36%	38%	38%	37%	38%	38%	38%	40%
85	2.7	5.3	7.1	9.0	9.9	10.	11.	13.	14.
85	35%	35%	37%	37%	37%	37%	39%	39%	38%
84	3.0	5.6	7.3	8.9	9.8	10.	11.	13.	14.
84	35%	37%	40%	38%	38%	39%	41%	40%	40%
83	3.7	6.4	8.2	9.7	10.	12.	13.	14.	15.
83	34%	37%	37%	37%	38%	39%	38%	38%	37%
82	4.0	6.7	8.4	9.5	11.	12.	13.	13.	15.
82	38%	40%	40%	40%	41%	40%	40%	39%	38%
81	4.6	7.3	8.6	10.	12.	12.	13.	15.	16.
81	39%	41%	41%	40%	40%	41%	40%	37%	39%
80	5.1	7.8	9.3	11.	11.	12.	13.	15.	17.
80	40%	40%	40%	40%	40%	40%	40%	40%	40%
79	5.8	8.5	10.	11.	12.	13.	14.	16.	17.
79	39%	41%	41%	40%	40%	41%	40%	37%	39%
78	6.6	8.6	10.	11.	13.	14.	15.	16.	17.
78	38%	40%	40%	40%	41%	40%	40%	39%	38%
77	7.5	9.5	11.	12.	14.	15.	16.	17.	18.
77	34%	37%	37%	37%	38%	39%	38%	38%	37%
76	8.4	10.	12.	13.	15.	16.	16.	17.	19.
76	35%	37%	40%	38%	38%	39%	41%	40%	40%
75	8.9	11.	12.	14.	16.	16.	17.	19.	20.
75	35%	35%	37%	37%	37%	37%	39%	39%	38%

HIGH PRICE PUT TABLE
Exercise Price is (90)

Average Volatility

STOCK PRICE — NUMBER OF MONTHS BEFORE THE OPTIONS EXPIRE

STOCK PRICE	1	2	3	4	5	6	7	8	9
105	0.0	0.2	0.8	1.7	2.4	3.1	3.7	4.5	5.3
105	3%	23%	30%	38%	39%	40%	40%	42%	41%
104	0.0	0.5	1.3	2.2	3.1	3.7	4.4	5.3	6.1
104	6%	24%	28%	34%	36%	38%	38%	38%	36%
103	0.0	0.5	1.3	2.3	3.1	3.7	4.4	5.1	6.0
103	9%	27%	39%	41%	42%	42%	42%	42%	42%
102	0.0	0.8	1.8	2.8	3.8	4.6	5.2	6.0	6.8
102	13%	28%	35%	37%	39%	38%	39%	36%	37%
101	0.0	0.9	1.9	3.0	3.9	4.5	5.2	6.0	6.8
101	18%	39%	41%	42%	41%	41%	42%	42%	41%
100	0.2	1.5	2.5	3.6	4.6	5.3	6.0	6.7	7.6
100	25%	36%	39%	38%	38%	37%	36%	37%	33%
99	0.3	1.4	2.5	3.7	4.5	5.3	5.8	6.7	7.6
99	27%	43%	44%	42%	42%	42%	43%	42%	39%
98	0.6	2.1	3.2	4.4	5.4	6.0	6.7	7.5	8.6
98	33%	40%	40%	36%	33%	36%	33%	35%	34%
97	0.8	2.2	3.3	4.5	5.4	6.2	6.8	7.6	8.6
97	40%	42%	43%	40%	40%	38%	38%	38%	36%
96	1.1	2.8	4.0	5.2	6.2	7.0	7.7	8.5	9.0
96	39%	41%	37%	33%	34%	33%	35%	35%	38%
95	1.4	3.0	4.2	5.3	6.3	7.0	7.7	8.5	8.9
95	44%	42%	42%	37%	36%	37%	38%	39%	40%
94	1.9	3.6	4.8	6.2	7.1	7.9	8.6	8.8	9.7
94	41%	33%	34%	35%	36%	36%	38%	37%	37%
93	2.1	3.8	5.0	6.3	7.2	7.9	8.6	8.7	9.6
93	44%	40%	36%	39%	41%	41%	41%	42%	42%
92	2.6	4.5	5.8	7.0	8.0	8.6	9.5	9.5	11.
92	34%	34%	36%	38%	40%	40%	40%	41%	43%
91	3.0	4.8	6.1	7.3	8.3	8.5	9.4	10.	11.
91	36%	39%	41%	42%	43%	42%	43%	43%	44%
90	3.7	5.6	6.8	8.1	8.5	9.3	10.	11.	11.
90	34%	40%	41%	42%	42%	41%	40%	41%	42%
89	4.3	6.2	7.3	8.5	9.4	10.	10.	11.	12.
89	36%	39%	41%	42%	43%	42%	43%	43%	44%
88	5.3	7.0	8.3	9.4	10.	11.	11.	12.	13.
88	34%	34%	36%	38%	40%	40%	40%	41%	43%
87	6.1	7.8	8.7	9.5	10.	11.	12.	12.	13.
87	44%	40%	36%	39%	41%	41%	41%	42%	42%
86	7.1	8.8	9.6	10.	12.	12.	12.	13.	15.
86	41%	33%	34%	35%	36%	36%	38%	37%	37%
85	8.0	9.0	10.	11.	12.	13.	13.	14.	15.
85	44%	42%	42%	37%	36%	37%	38%	39%	40%

High Volatility

STOCK PRICE — NUMBER OF MONTHS BEFORE THE OPTIONS EXPIRE

STOCK PRICE	1	2	3	4	5	6	7	8	9
105	0.3	2.2	4.0	6.0	7.4	8.5	9.4	10.	11.
105	19%	33%	35%	32%	32%	33%	34%	36%	35%
104	0.6	2.7	4.6	6.6	8.1	9.1	9.8	11.	12.
104	24%	31%	32%	33%	31%	33%	34%	34%	33%
103	0.7	2.9	4.7	6.8	8.2	9.3	9.7	11.	12.
103	27%	35%	35%	33%	34%	35%	36%	36%	36%
102	1.0	3.4	5.4	7.6	8.9	9.6	10.	12.	14.
102	29%	31%	32%	31%	33%	35%	35%	33%	35%
101	1.1	3.7	5.6	7.7	9.2	9.5	10.	12.	14.
101	35%	35%	32%	33%	35%	35%	38%	36%	37%
100	1.5	4.2	6.3	8.4	9.4	10.	11.	13.	15.
100	34%	32%	31%	32%	35%	35%	37%	36%	33%
99	1.6	4.4	6.4	8.6	9.3	11.	12.	13.	14.
99	37%	35%	34%	35%	37%	37%	39%	37%	36%
98	2.2	5.0	7.2	9.2	10.	12.	12.	13.	15.
98	35%	32%	31%	37%	35%	35%	35%	34%	36%
97	2.4	5.4	7.4	9.1	10.	11.	12.	14.	15.
97	36%	33%	36%	38%	40%	37%	35%	39%	38%
96	2.9	6.0	8.1	9.9	11.	12.	13.	15.	17.
96	33%	33%	35%	37%	36%	35%	35%	38%	38%
95	3.3	6.2	8.3	9.8	11.	12.	13.	15.	17.
95	36%	36%	39%	37%	35%	36%	39%	39%	40%
94	3.9	7.1	8.8	10.	12.	13.	15.	15.	17.
94	33%	35%	39%	34%	35%	35%	38%	37%	38%
93	4.2	7.3	8.7	11.	12.	14.	14.	16.	17.
93	35%	40%	41%	37%	38%	40%	40%	40%	40%
92	4.8	7.9	9.5	12.	13.	14.	15.	17.	19.
92	34%	40%	35%	37%	38%	38%	40%	40%	37%
91	5.3	8.5	10.	12.	13.	14.	15.	17.	18.
91	38%	42%	37%	40%	42%	41%	42%	40%	35%
90	6.0	8.5	11.	12.	14.	15.	17.	18.	19.
90	42%	36%	37%	39%	40%	40%	40%	36%	35%
89	6.7	9.4	11.	13.	15.	16.	16.	18.	20.
89	38%	42%	37%	40%	42%	41%	42%	40%	35%
88	7.5	10.	11.	14.	16.	16.	17.	19.	21.
88	34%	40%	35%	37%	38%	38%	40%	40%	37%
87	8.4	11.	12.	15.	16.	17.	18.	20.	21.
87	35%	40%	41%	37%	38%	40%	40%	40%	40%
86	8.8	12.	13.	16.	17.	18.	19.	21.	22.
86	33%	35%	39%	34%	35%	35%	38%	37%	38%
85	9.8	13.	14.	17.	17.	18.	20.	21.	22.
85	36%	36%	39%	37%	35%	36%	39%	39%	40%

HIGH PRICE PUT TABLE

Exercise Price is (100)

Average Volatility

STOCK PRICE — NUMBER OF MONTHS BEFORE THE OPTIONS EXPIRE

STOCK PRICE	1	2	3	4	5	6	7	8	9
115	0.0	0.5	1.4	2.4	3.3	4.1	4.7	5.6	6.5
115	8%	27%	38%	40%	42%	42%	42%	42%	42%
114	0.0	0.9	1.9	3.0	3.9	4.8	5.5	6.5	7.2
114	9%	27%	33%	36%	39%	37%	40%	36%	38%
113	0.0	0.9	2.0	3.0	4.0	4.8	5.4	6.4	7.2
113	15%	35%	40%	42%	41%	42%	42%	42%	42%
112	0.1	1.4	2.4	3.7	4.8	5.6	6.2	7.1	8.2
112	18%	33%	38%	38%	37%	37%	38%	37%	33%
111	0.2	1.4	2.6	3.8	4.9	5.6	6.2	7.2	8.2
111	26%	41%	42%	41%	41%	42%	43%	41%	38%
110	0.5	2.0	3.1	4.5	5.6	6.4	7.0	8.0	9.0
110	27%	36%	40%	38%	36%	34%	37%	33%	33%
109	0.6	2.0	3.2	4.5	5.5	6.3	7.0	7.9	8.9
109	37%	44%	42%	42%	41%	42%	43%	41%	37%
108	1.0	2.6	3.9	5.3	6.3	7.1	7.8	8.9	9.1
108	37%	40%	38%	35%	35%	34%	34%	33%	35%
107	1.1	2.8	4.1	5.4	6.4	7.3	7.9	9.0	10.
107	41%	42%	42%	40%	39%	37%	38%	37%	39%
106	1.6	3.4	4.7	6.1	7.2	8.1	8.8	9.9	10.
106	41%	39%	33%	33%	33%	35%	35%	38%	37%
105	1.7	3.6	4.9	6.2	7.3	8.2	8.8	9.8	10.
105	43%	42%	38%	37%	36%	37%	39%	39%	40%
104	2.3	4.3	5.6	7.0	8.2	8.8	9.7	10.	11.
104	41%	32%	33%	36%	35%	37%	37%	38%	38%
103	2.6	4.5	5.8	7.1	8.3	8.7	9.6	10.	11.
103	43%	38%	36%	40%	43%	42%	42%	42%	42%
102	3.2	5.2	6.5	7.9	8.6	9.5	10.	11.	12.
102	36%	34%	36%	41%	41%	41%	41%	42%	41%
101	3.6	5.4	6.9	8.3	8.5	9.4	10.	11.	12.
101	36%	39%	41%	42%	42%	43%	45%	42%	44%
100	4.2	6.2	7.6	8.5	10.	11.	11.	12.	13.
100	35%	40%	41%	41%	42%	41%	41%	41%	42%
99	4.7	6.8	8.1	9.4	10.	11.	11.	12.	13.
99	36%	39%	41%	42%	42%	43%	45%	42%	44%
98	5.7	7.7	8.6	10.	11.	11.	12.	13.	15.
98	36%	34%	36%	41%	41%	41%	41%	42%	41%
97	6.5	8.4	9.5	10.	12.	12.	12.	14.	15.
97	43%	38%	36%	40%	43%	42%	42%	42%	42%
96	7.5	8.8	10.	11.	12.	13.	14.	15.	16.
96	41%	32%	33%	36%	35%	37%	37%	38%	38%
95	8.4	9.8	11.	12.	13.	13.	14.	15.	17.
95	43%	42%	38%	37%	36%	37%	39%	39%	40%

High Volatility

STOCK PRICE — NUMBER OF MONTHS BEFORE THE OPTIONS EXPIRE

STOCK PRICE	1	2	3	4	5	6	7	8	9
115	0.7	3.1	5.1	7.4	8.9	9.7	10.	12.	14.
115	26%	33%	34%	33%	33%	34%	36%	35%	37%
114	1.0	3.6	5.7	8.0	9.6	10.	11.	13.	15.
114	26%	31%	32%	31%	33%	34%	35%	34%	35%
113	1.1	3.8	5.9	8.2	9.6	10.	11.	13.	15.
113	31%	34%	34%	34%	37%	35%	36%	36%	38%
112	1.5	4.4	6.6	8.9	10.	11.	12.	14.	16.
112	31%	32%	33%	33%	34%	35%	34%	35%	33%
111	1.6	4.7	6.8	9.1	10.	11.	13.	14.	16.
111	35%	34%	35%	36%	36%	35%	37%	38%	35%
110	2.1	5.2	7.4	9.3	11.	12.	14.	14.	17.
110	35%	32%	32%	35%	34%	35%	34%	35%	34%
109	2.3	5.4	7.6	9.2	11.	12.	13.	15.	17.
109	37%	34%	33%	37%	37%	39%	37%	35%	39%
108	2.8	6.2	8.4	10.	11.	13.	14.	16.	18.
108	35%	33%	34%	35%	36%	35%	35%	35%	36%
107	3.1	6.4	8.6	10.	12.	13.	14.	16.	18.
107	36%	34%	37%	40%	37%	35%	37%	38%	39%
106	3.6	7.1	9.0	11.	13.	14.	15.	17.	18.
106	34%	32%	37%	39%	34%	35%	35%	38%	37%
105	4.0	7.3	8.9	11.	13.	14.	16.	16.	19.
105	34%	35%	40%	38%	35%	38%	39%	40%	40%
104	4.6	8.1	9.7	12.	14.	15.	16.	18.	20.
104	31%	35%	40%	35%	35%	35%	38%	39%	38%
103	4.9	8.4	10.	12.	14.	15.	16.	18.	20.
103	36%	40%	37%	38%	39%	40%	41%	41%	40%
102	5.6	8.6	11.	13.	14.	16.	17.	19.	20.
102	35%	41%	35%	38%	38%	38%	40%	40%	36%
101	6.0	9.4	11.	13.	15.	17.	18.	19.	21.
101	38%	41%	38%	42%	42%	41%	42%	40%	35%
100	6.8	10.	11.	14.	16.	17.	18.	20.	22.
100	41%	36%	39%	40%	40%	40%	40%	36%	35%
99	7.3	10.	12.	15.	16.	17.	18.	20.	22.
99	38%	41%	38%	42%	42%	41%	42%	40%	35%
98	8.3	11.	13.	16.	17.	18.	20.	21.	23.
98	35%	41%	35%	38%	38%	38%	40%	40%	36%
97	8.7	12.	14.	16.	17.	19.	20.	21.	23.
97	36%	40%	37%	38%	39%	40%	41%	41%	40%
96	9.7	12.	15.	17.	19.	20.	21.	22.	25.
96	31%	35%	40%	35%	35%	35%	38%	39%	38%
95	10.	13.	15.	17.	19.	21.	21.	23.	25.
95	34%	35%	40%	38%	35%	38%	39%	40%	40%

Index

About the Author

Kenneth R. Trester is recognized as a leading international options advisor. He is a popular speaker at financial conventions and options trading seminars and has even given seminars in Russia. Through his market letters, he has originated many of the options strategies that are industry standards today.

Ken Trester is the author of *The Complete Option Player*, now in its 5th edition. It was followed by *The Option Players Advanced Guidebook* and *101 Option Trading Secrets*. Other works include a comprehensive options home study course, *Secrets to Stock Option Success*, and software for options trading, *Option Master*®, *The Push-Button Option Trader* and *The Push-Button Option Writer*. He has written numerous articles that have been quoted in such publications as *Barrons* and is a contributing author to the *Encyclopedia of Stock Market Techniques*. Ken Trester also coauthored the book, *Complete Business BASIC Programming*. Besides, Ken Trester is the editor of *The Put & Call Tactician* Advisory Service.

Ken Trester has been trading options since the options exchanges first opened in 1973. His background combines systems analysis, operations research and investment management. He has been the president of a management consulting firm and an Assistant Professor of Management at the California State University, Fresno and in the Computer Science Department at Golden West College. He holds a B.S. and M.B.A. from Utah State University and has done post graduate work at the University of Oregon.

Please Send Me Information on the Following Products and Services:

Option Market Letter: _____ Put & Call Tactician

Books: _____ The Complete Option Player

_____ The Option Player's
Advanced Guidebook

Option Software &
Other Products: _____ Computer Software—
Option Trading

_____ Options Home Study Course

_____ How to Buy Stock and Commodity
Options—Video Tape

Option Seminars: _____ Option Trading Camps

_____ Option Trading Camp Videos

NAME _____

MAILING ADDRESS _____

CITY, STATE & ZIP CODE_____

Institute for Options Research, Inc.
Fax: 1-775-588-8481 or call: 1-800-407-2422

Purchasers of THE COMPLETE OPTION PLAYER are eligible to receive a FREE copy of one issue of Kenneth R. Trester's Options Newsletter. To receive your FREE copy, simply fill in and mail this coupon.

NAME _____

MAILING ADDRESS _____

CITY, STATE & ZIP CODE_____

Return To:
Institute for Options Research, Inc.
Fax: 1-775-588-8481
Internet: GoOptions.com